Taking the Step Up to Supervisor

Geoff Nichols

American Media Publishing
4900 University Avenue
West Des Moines, Iowa 50266-6769 U.S.A.
800/262-2557

Taking the Step Up to Supervisor

Geoff Nichols

Credits:

American Media Publishing:	Art Bauer
	Todd McDonald
Managing Editor:	Karen Massetti Miller
Designer:	Gayle O'Brien
Cover Design:	Polly Beaver

Published by American Media Inc.
4900 University Avenue
West Des Moines, IA 50266-6769

Library of Congress Card Number 97-77106
Nichols, Geoff
Taking the Step Up to Supervisor

Printed in the United States of America
ISBN 1-884926-84-3

Introduction

Becoming a supervisor is your first step in the challenging and rewarding field of management. You have earned a new level of responsibility and authority because of your technical skills, attitude, and potential. Now you must master different skills to help you continue to advance and grow. This book will help you do that.

Management is still more art than science; however, the basic skills necessary to succeed have been clearly identified and can be learned. As with any new set of skills, it is best to follow the instructions closely at first. But then, as you gain more confidence, try your own methods and discover what works best for you. This will allow you to develop your ability to its highest level.

Above all, relax and enjoy the challenge. You have reached a significant level of achievement and growth. Now you can watch those whom you supervise achieve and grow and know that you helped them do so. That is one of the greatest rewards of being a supervisor. Good luck!

About the Author

With 21 years of management experience, Geoff Nichols has built a solid base of knowledge in recruitment, performance management, employment law, training, industrial safety, presentation skills, direct sales, and direct marketing. He has served as a human resources executive in manufacturing, banking, and health care.

As an executive for the world's largest business training organization for 10 years, Mr. Nichols built a staff of trainers, managers, sales representatives, and support personnel that delivered more than 9,000 public and private business seminars each year in the U.S., Canada, and Europe.

As a consultant for the past five years, Mr. Nichols has trained thousands of supervisors, managers, human resource professionals, sales professionals, and executives in all types of industries throughout North America and England. This broad experience plus a B.A. in psychology and an M.S. in industrial safety give Mr. Nichols a strong foundation for helping people be more effective in their jobs.

Self-Assessment

How do you rate your supervisory ability? This self-assessment will allow you to identify skill areas in which you are strong and those in which you can develop. This will help guide you to the chapters in the book that will provide the quickest and greatest value.

Read each statement and then circle the number that most closely describes your current skill level according the following scale: 1 = Strongly disagree, 2 = Disagree, 3 = Not sure, 4 = Agree, 5 = Strongly agree. Be honest with yourself as you answer the questions.

1. I am comfortable in the role of a supervisor and understand how I can best carry out all of my duties.	1	2	3	4	5
2. I am able to command respect from everyone I work with in my role as a supervisor.	1	2	3	4	5
3. I know what my employees are looking for from me and their jobs.	1	2	3	4	5
4. I know how to help employees give their best efforts to their jobs.	1	2	3	4	5
5. I know how to get my employees to work together as a team.	1	2	3	4	5
6. I always listen well to understand the other person's viewpoint before I offer mine.	1	2	3	4	5
7. I am always careful to watch what I say and how I speak when talking to others.	1	2	3	4	5
8. I know which words are likely to provoke anger in others.	1	2	3	4	5

9. I know how much time to spend in gathering information before making decisions. 1 2 3 4 5

10. I know how find the root causes of problems. 1 2 3 4 5

11. I am aware of the main reasons conflicts occur in the workplace and how to minimize them. 1 2 3 4 5

12. I am confident in my ability to resolve conflict between two of my employees. 1 2 3 4 5

13. I am comfortable in disciplining my employees. 1 2 3 4 5

14. I know why documentation of employee behavior problems needs to be done and how to do it well. 1 2 3 4 5

15. I have a good understanding of the major employment laws and how to avoid problems with them. 1 2 3 4 5

16. I am well organized and have little difficulty handling my workload. 1 2 3 4 5

17. I know how my time is spent on the job and rarely procrastinate or get into time crunches. 1 2 3 4 5

18. I rarely feel over stressed on the job and generally feel positive and optimistic about my career. 1 2 3 4 5

19. I understand which are the biggest stressors in my life and have a plan to deal with them. 1 2 3 4 5

20. I have a clear idea of what it takes to advance up through the management ranks. 1 2 3 4 5

Now, add up the numbers you circled and compare your total to the table below:

- **60 or less**—You have taken a good first step in developing yourself as a supervisor and preparing yourself for future advancement. Focus on your five lowest-rated statements and then review the Table of Contents to find the chapters that will help you develop in these areas. Start by reading these chapters, then go on to others according to your interest and needs.

- **61 to 80**—You already have a good understanding of your job as a supervisor. Look at your lowest-rated statements and begin reading the book by focusing first on the chapters that address these issues. Then go on to others according to your interest and needs.

- **81 to 100**—You are very confident in your understanding of your job as a supervisor. Focus on your lowest-rated statements and begin reading the book by reviewing the chapters that address these issues. Refer to other chapters as you need to when challenges arise in these areas.

Whatever rating you achieved, you have started a positive process of development to gain the knowledge and skills you need to progress in your career and your life. No book can give you all the answers because supervision is as much an art as it is a science. However, this will give you a good map with some specific directions to take which will help you go where you want to go. Good luck!

Chapter *One*

Learning Your New Role

Chapter Objectives

- Explain how the supervisor's job differs from that of a nonsupervisor or manager.
- Become familiar with your new responsibilities as a supervisor and the new personal skills you will need to develop.
- Anticipate the benefits as well as the typical challenges of being a supervisor.

Do you remember when you were hired for your first full-time job? For many of us, it was both exciting and, at the same time, somewhat frightening. It was our first opportunity to demonstrate our abilities and see how we measured up in the "real world." We soon learned that we could do the job and do it well.

Becoming a supervisor is much like getting your first job.

Becoming a supervisor is much like getting that first job. In fact, it is a new and different job! Your responsibility now is not only to do your own tasks, but also to get work done through other people. In a very real way, your success lies in their hands! This can again be exciting and frightening, but you will find that you can do it well and will one day want to step up into management.

The main differences in each of these career steps are the scope and depth of their duties. *Scope* refers to the different kinds of tasks you must do, and *depth* refers to their difficulty and impact on the organization. The higher in the organization you go, the greater the scope and depth of your duties. The diagram on the next page shows how each step differs.

Comparison of Organizational Roles

Manager

- Plans work for department.
- Assigns tasks/objectives to supervisors and others.
- Evaluates others' work.
- Sets department policies.
- Sets department budget within given guidelines.
- Has higher impact on organization's success.
- Responsible for results.

Supervisor

- Plans work for work group.
- Assigns tasks to others.
- Evaluates others' work.
- Carries out policies.
- Meets budget goals.
- Responsible for others' work.

Nonsupervisor

- Does work that is assigned.
- Has several main responsibilities.
- Exercises limited judgment.
- Evaluated for personal effort.

These are general descriptions of each career step. Different organizations define and title the various levels in their structures differently according to organization size, business, culture, etc. Sometimes one level may have a mix of tasks from higher or lower levels as described above.

Becoming a supervisor for the first time is truly like getting a new job. And with a new job at a higher level, you can expect a new set of benefits and challenges.

Anticipating New Challenges and Benefits

Becoming a supervisor brings with it a wide range of new experiences.

Becoming a supervisor brings with it a wide range of new experiences. Many are very positive and fulfilling, such as:

- Increased status.
- Increased authority.
- Increased compensation.
- Increased visibility in the organization.
- Ability to make a more important contribution to the organization.
- Seeing people grow and earn promotions as a result of your coaching.
- Satisfaction of leading a team to achieve results.
- Greater involvement in other areas of the organization.
- Greater opportunity for personal and professional growth.
- Greater feelings of success.

You can probably think of other positive effects that are indirect reflections of your new job as supervisor. These might include the ability to buy items you have long wanted or to make progress toward your financial goals. Or they may be more personal, such as the look of pride you see in your family's eyes as they see you make progress in life.

Take a Moment

Write down what your new job as a supervisor means to you. This is a personal celebration of your accomplishment and a letter to yourself that you can look back on in the future. It's your time to recognize yourself!

____

____

____

As you take each new step in your career, remember to take some time to celebrate your success. This will help bring even more enjoyment to your achievements. It will also give you confidence as you approach new responsibilities.

Acquiring New Responsibilities and Skills

Some of your new responsibilities are similar to what you did before you became supervisor, but many are very different. Up to now, you have been responsible for developing your technical skills, assuring the quality your own work, and working well with others. From this point forward, you are faced with additional responsibilities that include:

- Coaching and motivating employees.
- Getting employees to work together as a team.
- Solving problems with others.
- Managing conflicts between others.
- Counseling and disciplining.
- Managing your time as well as that of others.
- Conducting meetings.
- Dealing with your stress and the stress of others.

These new responsibilities can be trying. In Chapter 8, we will discuss ways to deal effectively with stress; however, there are some unique challenges to being a new supervisor that we should address. Following are four of the most common challenges many new supervisors face and suggestions to help resolve the issues. Take a moment to review the list and highlight phrases that will help you.

Challenge	Suggestion
◆ Feeling overwhelmed	◆ Identify specifically what the issues are that seem too large and write them down. Analyze them to see if training or better time management will help or if something else is the problem. Look at both personal and organizational issues. Talk with your manager or some other experienced person who can offer advice. Understand that this is a common feeling for new supervisors.
◆ Jealousy from former coworkers	◆ Realize that it really is not personal. They would be jealous of anyone who took your job. Try asking for their opinions. If they seem resistant, talk with them individually and bring up the issue. Recognize their abilities and ask for their support. Be friendly, but don't try too hard. If they do not lessen their unpleasant behavior, document it. If it becomes disruptive, you may have to begin counseling and discipline.

◆ Lack of respect	◆ This may be resentment because you do things differently or want to make changes. If so, make sure your approach is well grounded; then be patient, show the benefits of your methods, and be open to good suggestions from others. Also, look at yourself to see if you might appear overly aggressive, defensive, or perhaps unassertive. Seek advice about this from someone you respect. Strive to come across as positive, confident, and reasonable in dealing with others at all levels.
◆ Frustration with bureaucracy	◆ Each organization has policies and procedures to ensure proper functioning, compliance with laws, fairness, etc. Sometimes they can seem tedious and restrictive. Make sure you understand the purpose of any policy you feel is a problem and offer alternatives in a positive way. Expect change to be slow and resisted by some people. All organizations have some bureaucracy, and not all of it can be changed. Stay patient, persistent, and positive.

Take a Moment

Are you facing any of the challenges just listed? List some positive steps you can take to deal with them below.

____

____

____

You may be faced with other challenges now or in the future. This book will help you be able to meet them effectively and with grace. Try to view each challenge as yet another opportunity to learn and grow, and it will seem less troubling. Good luck in your new job as a supervisor. It is a wonderful experience that can lead to even greater ones.

Chapter Summary

As you take the step up to supervisor, you will discover that the scope and depth of your duties will grow as you progress higher in your organization. As supervisor, your new duties will include planning work for your work group, assigning tasks to others, evaluating others' work, carrying out policies, meeting budget goals, and taking responsibility for the work of others.

To accomplish these duties, you will be taking on a variety of new responsibilities, including:

- Coaching and motivating employees.
- Getting employees to work together as a team.
- Solving problems with others.
- Managing conflicts between others.
- Counseling and disciplining.
- Managing your time as well as that of others.
- Conducting meetings.
- Dealing with your stress and the stress of others.

These new responsibilities can be challenging. Four common challenges faced by new supervisors include:

- Feeling overwhelmed.
- Jealousy from former coworkers.
- Lack of respect.
- Frustration with bureaucracy.

Viewing each new challenge as an opportunity to work and grow will make it seem less troubling.

Self-Check: Chapter 1 Review

Answers to the following questions may be found on page 120.

1. The higher in the organization you go, the greater the

   ________________________ and ______________________ of your duties.

2. Match the following organizational roles to their responsibilities:

   ______ Nonsupervisor

   ______ Supervisor

   ______ Manager

   a. Plans work for work group. Assigns tasks to others. Carries out policies. Meets budget goals. Responsible for others' work.

   b. Plans work for department. Assigns tasks/objectives. Sets department policies. Sets department budget within given guidelines. Responsible for results.

   c. Does work that is assigned. Has several main responsibilities. Exercises limited judgment. Evaluated for personal effort.

3. List three new responsibilities that come with the job of supervisor.

   a. ____

   b. ____

   c. ____

4. What are the four most common challenges faced by new supervisors?

   a. ______________________________

   b. ______________________________

   c. ______________________________

   d. ______________________________

Chapter *Two*

Motivating and Coaching Others

Chapter Objectives

- Explain the basics of motivation.
- Follow simple steps for coaching your employees.
- Develop a strong team.

Motivation is one of the most written-about topics in business. Sometimes it can seem confusing because there is a question as to whether a supervisor can actually *motivate* an employee or simply *support* whatever level of motivation the employee chooses to have.

Motivating Your Employees

Supervisors need to provide employees with good reasons to do their jobs in the best and fastest way.

Let's look at it practically. In its simplest terms, *motivation* can be defined as a reason to take action. The supervisor's responsibility in motivating employees really focuses on providing them with good reasons to do their jobs in the best and fastest way.

Money incentives are thought by some to be the best motivators. Although they can be effective, they have a major drawback: They are short-term. They are effective only for the time they are given. They build no continuing reason for employees to perform at their best.

Fear is also thought by some to be a good motivator. But it has a similar drawback: It is effective only as long as the supervisor is immediately present. If he or she is gone, productivity tends to decrease. Here again, there is no continuing reason for employees to give their best efforts.

So what are good motivators—good reasons for employees to perform well that are long-term and positive? These come from within employees themselves. They involve internal factors, such as pride, involvement, recognition of achievement, and the feeling of being treated with fairness and respect. The supervisor's job is to find ways to help employees have these experiences.

This can be difficult because each person is unique with his or her own set of needs, expectations, and goals. Yet there are some basic principles that apply to virtually everyone. Here are four proven guidelines that will influence employees to perform well:

- Show employees that they are important.
- Help employees meet their needs.
- Recognize employee achievements with awards.
- Treat employees fairly and consistently.

Showing Employees That They Are Important

Employees respond amazingly well when supervisors give them encouragement and show appreciation for their work. What's more, these actions take very little time and can cost little or nothing. Here are some ideas to consider:

Employees respond amazingly well when supervisors give them encouragement and show appreciation for their work.

- Give employees sincere compliments on their work. Be specific, keep it short, and smile! For example, "Bob, nice job on the Jones report. The writing and graphics were great, and you completed it ahead of time. Thanks!" This will help Bob feel that he is well regarded by someone who is important in his life—his supervisor. Most people appreciate this type of praise and will work as hard or harder to have it repeated. The positive effect can be enhanced by writing your compliment on the report or in a card and noting the event so you can bring it up later in a performance evaluation.

- Ask employees for their opinions on business issues. Everyone has an opinion and appreciates the opportunity to express it—especially to the boss.

- Give employees special projects. Make sure it's a project they can do, perhaps with a little coaching. Make it something that will help them to develop and learn something new.
- Communicate about what's going on. Tell them how the department or organization is doing—whether or not it's meeting its goals and what new things are coming up. Employees are very interested and greatly appreciate hearing this kind of information.
- Cross-train employees in other jobs. This not only makes their work more interesting, it gives them a broader perspective and makes them more valuable to the organization.
- Set goals with individuals about their performance and their development. Goal setting is one of the most powerful motivators. Helping employees to improve and grow is a strong, positive action that will get a strong, positive response.

Take a Moment

Select at least two of the ideas just listed, and plan how you can use them at your next opportunity.

____

____

____

____

____

____

Helping Employees Meet Their Needs

■ "I just don't know how to motivate my employees," Randy told Ahmed over lunch. "I try to give them the things I wanted as an employee, but it just isn't working."

"Maybe their needs are different than yours were," Ahmed responded. "Why don't you talk with them and try to find out what *they're* looking for."

Employees have a variety of needs that they hope to fulfill through their work, and those needs vary greatly. One of the factors that can influence an individual's needs is that individual's *personality type.*

A *personality type* is simply a way of categorizing personality traits that groups of people share. A number of well-researched personality profiles describe four distinct personality types, and each one has its own set of needs. People are always a unique mix of all four types; however, they tend to show the traits of one style most often. Here is a chart of the four styles, their traits, and the needs that each is generally trying to fulfill.

Style	Traits	Needs
Forceful	Confident, bold, opinionated	Control, status, task accomplishment, directness
Social	Likable, persuasive, outgoing, optimistic	Involvement with other people, to talk, to be liked
Steady	Controlled, patient, conscientious, pleasant	Well-defined structure/procedures, stability, ample time to change
Detailed	Accurate, logical, quality-focused	Specific facts, attention to detail, time to analyze and think, task orientation

Take a Moment

Consider your own personality. You have your own unique mix of traits and needs—think of the ones you have most of the time at work. Write down the style that best describes you and which needs are most important to you.

____

____

____

Now consider one of your best employees. Write down the style that best describes him or her. Then write down the needs he or she seems to have and how you could help the employee fulfill them. For example: "Barbara: She seems to predominantly have the Forceful style. She needs control and accomplishment. I could put her in charge of the office more."

____

____

____

____

On a separate sheet of paper, do the same for each of your employees. This information plus what they have shared with you about their expectations give you the ability to motivate your employees by helping them fulfill their personal needs at work. If you're not sure about any of your employees, ask them what style fits them best and what their needs are. Getting their involvement is in itself motivating and will help you to get more commitment, loyalty, and productivity from them.

Recognizing Employee Achievements with Awards

Items like certificates, inexpensive plaques or trophies, coffee cups, lunches, a small amount of paid time off, etc., are effective, low-cost ways of reinforcing excellent performance. Involve your employees in setting performance goals and awards. Make sure that everyone can win but that they have to stretch to do it.

Also, make it fun! Once the goal has been achieved, you might have a celebration or a drawing in which employees receive prizes of approximately equal value. Employees also like having fun at their supervisor's expense. Promise them that if they achieve the goal, you'll wear a red fright wig, an ugly tie, or something else that is silly for a day or even just an hour. This allows them to enjoy their accomplishment and advertise it to others in the organization at the same time. It also shows a supervisor who is proud of the team and confident in him or herself.

Take a Moment

Write down three ideas for recognizing employee achievements with awards that you can put into use as soon as possible.

____

____

____

____

Treating Employees Fairly and Consistently

■ "Off to the golf course again," Nancy muttered as Dave and Jerry walked out the door. Dave and Jerry had been best friends when they were coworkers, and now that Dave was a supervisor, it seemed that the two of them were always slipping off for a "meeting" on the fairway. "I wonder why I bother to do my job at all?" Nancy asked herself. "Maybe it's time to start looking for a new one."

Nothing kills an employee's motivation quicker than seeing another employee benefit from favoritism.

Nothing kills an employee's motivation quicker than seeing another employee benefit from favoritism. This can be a real pitfall for a new supervisor because some of the employees he or she is now supervising were once coworkers and may still be personal friends. Be sure that all of your personnel decisions are unbiased by personal relationships.

Motivation is a key element in supervising people; however, it is just one part. Employees also look to their supervisor to provide coaching in how they can improve their job performance and work well with others.

Being a Good Coach and Team Leader

As we saw in Chapter 1, coaching is one of the new responsibilities you'll be taking on as a supervisor. Just what does that involve? *Coaching* is essentially teaching. But it is more than just instruction in a particular skill or job. It's a personal approach that makes a strong connection between the people involved.

Think back to when you were growing up and participating in some kind of team or group activity, such as scouting, soccer, softball, debate, or a musical performance. Now think about the various coaches you had. Which ones were the best for you and why? They probably took personal interest in you, taught you new skills, and encouraged you to improve.

These good coaches from your past can be good role models for you now. Think about the traits that you admired most about them. These might include:

- Fairness
- Calmness
- A positive attitude
- Willingness to listen
- Patience
- Knowledge

How do you rate in these areas?

The first step in being a good coach is to make a candid self-assessment of where you need to develop. For example, if you normally are not very patient, you can focus on this while working with your employees and develop it into more of a strength.

Take a Moment

List the traits of the coaches you admired most below. Then circle those traits that you need to develop in order to better coach your employees.

____

____

____

Part of being a coach is working with your employees as a team. The use of teams in business has proven to be one of the most effective ways to improve productivity and morale. Here are three suggestions to help your employees work better together as a team:

- **Set teamwork goals together.** Goal setting was discussed earlier as a good individual motivator. This is also true with work teams. Common effort to define specific work goals helps pull coworkers together in a powerful way.

- **Hold regular meetings with the team.** Start by developing meeting rules of conduct with your team. These might include "Start on time, end on time," "No interrupting," or "No side conversations while someone is talking." This helps meetings run more smoothly—and quickly.

  Meetings can cover a range of topics, such as last week's progress toward goals, reports from team members about achievements and problems, the coming week's activities, etc. This is also a good time to brainstorm possible solutions to difficult problems. This might involve inviting guests from other teams or departments to help in the process.

- **Develop a team identity.** It is important for teams to have pride in their group. One way is to allow the team to name themselves. They may already be known as "Accounting" or "Marketing," but they may enjoy giving themselves a name like the "A-Team" or "Lean, Mean Machine." This helps develop a sense of specialness and team cohesiveness.

Motivating and coaching others are two of the greatest challenges in supervision. However, by following the suggestions in this chapter, you can make them two of your greatest strengths.

Chapter Summary

We can define *motivation* as giving employees good reasons to complete their tasks in the best and fastest way. Four suggestions for supervisors to try include:

- Showing employees they are important.
- Helping them meet their needs.
- Recognizing their achievements.
- Treating them fairly and consistently.

We can define *coaching* as teaching with a personal approach that makes a strong connection with employees. The traits of a good coach include:

- Fairness
- Calmness
- A positive attitude
- Willingness to listen
- Patience
- Knowledge

Part of being a coach is working with your employees as a team. Three suggestions for this are:

- Setting teamwork goals together.
- Holding regular team meetings.
- Developing a team identity.

Self-Check: Chapter 2 Review

Answers to the following questions appear on pages 120 and 121.

1. What are the drawbacks to money incentives and fear as motivators?

   ____

   ____

   ____

2. What are three ways to show employees they are important?

   ____

   ____

   ____

3. Match the following personality types with their primary needs:

   ______ Forceful

   ______ Social

   ______ Steady

   ______ Detailed

   a. Well-defined structure/procedures, stability, ample time to change

   b. Specific facts, attention to detail, time to analyze and think, task orientation

   c. Control, status, task accomplishment, directness

   d. Involvement with other people, to talk, to be liked

4. What are three low- or no-cost ways to recognize employee achievements?

   a. ______________________________

   b. ______________________________

   c. ______________________________

5. What are four traits of a good coach?

   a. ______________________________

   b. ______________________________

   c. ______________________________

   d. ______________________________

6. Name three ways to develop your employees into a team.

   a. ______________________________

   b. ______________________________

   c. ______________________________

Chapter *Three*

Developing Your Communication Skills

Chapter Objectives

- ▶ Listen more effectively.
- ▶ Communicate more effectively—both verbally and nonverbally.
- ▶ Adjust how you communicate based on personality types.
- ▶ Run effective meetings.

Working effectively with your employees means communicating effectively. This involves mastering a variety of skills, including:

- Listening actively.
- Choosing your words carefully.
- Using an appropriate tone of voice and vocal inflections.
- Using appropriate body language.
- Adjusting your communication style to the styles of others.

Learning to Listen

In his book *The Seven Habits of Highly Effective People,* Stephen Covey lists "Seek first to understand, then to be understood" as a key habit. This is excellent advice because it encourages us to listen to others so that we understand why they think, feel, and act as they do before we speak. This is a very effective way for a new supervisor to gain employees' confidence and trust.

Many experts make a distinction between hearing and active listening. *Hearing* involves the physical process that occurs when sound waves vibrate against our eardrums. *Active listening* occurs when we actively try to understand what the other person is saying.

Hearing involves the physical process that occurs when sound waves vibrate against our eardrums.

Are you an active listener? Following the 10 steps below can help you improve your listening skills and get to the heart of the other person's message.

1. Show your attentiveness by facing the speaker directly.
2. Show interest by maintaining eye contact with the speaker (experts recommend that you maintain eye contact at least 80 percent of the time).
3. Avoid prejudging the worthiness of the message based on the person's appearance, position, vocabulary, or pronunciation.
4. Listen primarily for the speaker's intent and what is important to him or her.
5. Avoid tuning out to prepare your response while the other person is speaking.
6. Ask questions to clarify the speaker's meaning.
7. Avoid interrupting the speaker.
8. Encourage the speaker by smiling or nodding your head.
9. Before answering, pause and consider the speaker's viewpoint and how to be tactful.
10. Avoid trying to have the last word.

Active listening occurs when we actively try to understand what the other person is saying.

Take a Moment

Answer the following 10 questions by putting a check in the appropriate box according to how a work associate who knows you well would honestly rate you.

	Not Often	Some-times	Mostly	Always
1. Do I prepare myself by facing the speaker directly?	❑	❑	❑	❑
2. Do I maintain eye contact 80 percent of the time?	❑	❑	❑	❑
3. Do I avoid prejudging the worthiness of the message based on the person's appearance, position, vocabulary, or pronuncia-tion?	❑	❑	❑	❑
4. Do I listen primarily for intent and what is important to the speaker?	❑	❑	❑	❑
5. Do I avoid tuning out to prepare my response while the other person is speaking?	❑	❑	❑	❑
6. Do I ask questions and clarify the speaker's meaning?	❑	❑	❑	❑
7. Do I avoid interrupting the speaker?	❑	❑	❑	❑
8. Do I encourage the speaker with a smile or head nodding?	❑	❑	❑	❑

Continued on next page

Take a Moment *(continued)*

	Not Often	Some-times	Mostly	Always
9. Before answering, do I pause and consider the speaker's viewpoint and how to be tactful?	❑	❑	❑	❑
10. Do I avoid trying to have the last word?	❑	❑	❑	❑

You may find it difficult to answer these questions from someone else's viewpoint, but doing so will help you see your listening skills from the perspective of others and develop those skills that need improvement. If you feel comfortable doing so, ask a work associate to answer the questions as well, and compare your answers. Look at those questions that you and/or your associate checked as Sometimes or Not Often and focus on developing those skills.

Communication always goes two ways. We focused on listening first to emphasize the need to actively listen to others before we respond to them. Now we will consider how we send information, beginning with the importance of making careful word choices.

Choosing the Right Words

■ Walden, a supervisor, had just observed Theresa close a sale and wanted to give her a few pointers, so he called her into his office.

"Theresa, I just watched you with that customer out there, and I'd like to give you some advice," he began. "You know what your problem is? You never give the customer time to ask questions. Instead, you always rush right to the close. You should try giving them a chance to talk—you'll make more sales that way."

Walden thought Theresa would be grateful for the feedback, but instead of thanking him for his comments, she simply excused herself and went back to her work.

"What's her problem?" Walden asked himself as he watched her walk away. "If she can't take a suggestion, she shouldn't be in this business. I'm going to have to talk to her about that bad attitude sometime."

When we talk with others, we can unintentionally provoke a negative reaction just by the words we choose.

When we talk with others, we can unintentionally provoke a negative reaction just by the words we choose. This is particularly important when we are having a serious conversation—perhaps in correcting or disciplining an employee. The following chart lists some of the most common problem words or phrases, many of which appear in the previous example, and more tactful alternatives you can use to avoid problems.

Problem Words/Phrases	Good Alternatives
• **Should** "You should/should not do that." Should conveys strong, mostly negative judgment.	• **Could or Would** As in "You could . . ." or "I would like you to . . ."
• **Always or Never** As in "You always . . ." or "You never . . ." These are absolutes and are generally exaggerations.	• **Often/Generally or Rarely** As in "You often . . ." or "You generally . . ." or "You rarely . . ."
• **Lazy, Bad Attitude, Defensive, etc.** Any name or label conveys negative judgment.	• **Describe the person's behavior.** For example, "Your work rate is slower than others'," or "You seem to disagree with most things I say."

Take a Moment

List some of the words or phrases you have heard that provoke a negative reaction from employees or from you. The more conscious you are of these kinds of language mistakes, the less likely it is that you will make them.

____

____

____

____

Another way to avoid communication problems is to use *I* or *my* phrases instead of starting sentences with *you.* This is perceived much less as a personal attack by the person hearing the comment. Here are some examples of how to make this change.

***You* Comment**	***I* or *My* Comment**
• "*You* need to spend more time checking these reports."	• "*I* am concerned about the number of errors in your work."
• "*You* shouldn't be doing that."	• "*I* prefer for that not to be done."
• "*You're* wrong."	• "*I* don't agree." or "That hasn't been *my* experience."

Take a Moment

Think about *you* phrases you have heard or used yourself recently. Write them down and then write alternative *I* or *my* phrases to replace them.

____

____

____

____

Although you should always give your employees your honest appraisal of their work, you will find they will be much more receptive to your suggestions if you choose words that are less likely to provoke anger and defensiveness. The same is true for the *way* you say things.

Using the Appropriate Tone of Voice

■ Raphael had just returned from lunch and was heading back into the work area. At the sound of his footsteps, Lucinda looked up from her desk. "Oh, it's you," she said, and looked back down again.

"I wonder what she meant by that," Raphael thought as he headed back to his desk.

When communicating with your employees, always pay attention to the sound of your words.

As important as word choice is, communication experts believe that *how* we speak is even more important. For example, the phrase "Oh, it's you" can mean "I expected someone else," "It's good to see you," "It's not good to see *you*," "I'm bored," and many other possibilities, depending on how you say it. When communicating with your employees, always pay attention to the sound of your words.

Several factors effect how you will be perceived by others, including:

- **Pitch**
  A high-pitched voice can be perceived as childlike or nervous, while a low-pitched voice is often perceived as authoritative. Pitch can be affected by stress, which tenses your vocal cords, making your pitch higher. Monitor your pitch during stressful situations; take deep breaths to help your vocal cords relax so you can maintain your normal pitch.

- **Volume**
  A loud voice is often associated with someone who is angry or overly aggressive; a voice that is too soft can be difficult to hear and suggests shyness. Practice maintaining a volume that is loud enough to be heard clearly, but not so loud that it's overpowering.

- **Quality**
  A nasal or sharp voice can be irritating to a listener; a smooth voice is often perceived as soothing.

- **Rate**
  Speaking too fast can make a person appear nervous or overly excited; speaking too slow can make the speaker appear uncertain of his or her message. Strive to maintain a steady, moderate rate of speech.

- **Emphasis**
  As we saw in our previous example, emphasizing words can change their meaning.

Communicating effectively means using your tone of voice to support your verbal message. For example, if you are trying to put an employee at ease for a performance evaluation, your pitch, volume, quality, and rate of speaking should work together to convey a calm mood. Likewise, if you want to inspire employees during a pep talk, you can increase your volume and rate of speech to convey excitement and enthusiasm.

Communicating effectively means using your tone of voice to support your verbal message.

Take a Moment

How do you sound to others? Tape-record yourself in a casual conversation (with the other person's permission), or ask a friend for his or her reactions.

Voice Pitch	high	medium	low
Voice Volume	loud	moderate	soft
Speech Rate	fast	moderate	slow
Voice Quality	sharp	smooth	nasal

We have seen that how you say something can work to support what you say. Another aspect of communication that can affect your message is how you look when you speak, or your *body language.*

Using Appropriate Body Language

As a manager, one of your goals is to build open communication with your employees. Gestures, posture, and facial expressions are all aspects of body language that can encourage open communication and support your spoken message.

Smiling can show employees that you are interested in them and what they have to say and encourage them to communicate with you.

One body language technique that can support your efforts at open communication is simply to *smile.* Smiling can show employees that you are interested in them and what they have to say and encourage them to communicate with you.

Here are four other body language techniques that can encourage communication:

- Leaning toward the other person sends a positive message—you are interested in what he or she has to say. Leaning back or tilting your head backward sends a negative message—one of disbelief or exerting power.

- Maintaining eye contact approximately 80 percent of the time also shows positive interest in the other person. Little eye contact sends a negative message, such as shiftiness, shame, or lack of truthfulness.

- Relaxed arms and open hands send the positive message that you are open to the other person. Folded arms and closed or pointed fingers send a negative message of closed-mindedness or desire to intimidate.

- Sitting directly across from someone sends the positive message that you wish to communicate without barriers. Sitting behind a desk sends a negative message—one of being aloof or demonstrating power.

Consistency in your words, the sound of your voice, and your body language helps keep communication clear and reduces misunderstandings.

Consistency in your words, the sound of your voice, and your body language helps keep communication clear and reduces misunderstandings. There is one more factor that can help you communicate effectively—adjusting your communication to the personality type of your listener.

Adjusting to Different Personality Types

In Chapter 2, we discussed the four different personality types. We also noted that although each of us is a unique mix of all four types, we tend to display the traits of one type more than the others. Each type also prefers to communicate in its own way. Here is a guide to help in communicating with the different types you work with:

Each personality type prefers to communicate in its own way.

- **Forceful**
  Come to the point quickly and be brief. Offer alternatives on how to complete a task in the quickest way. Don't go into details unless they ask or specific procedures are required. Speak confidently and use statements starting with *I* and *My.*

- **Social**
  Smile and show that you are friendly. Ask for their help. Be brief in your statements, and don't go into details unless they are necessary. Ask their opinion and allow them time to talk. Use their name and *you* in your comments. Set deadlines.

- **Steady**
  Smile and show that you are friendly. Ask for their help. Give details and ask for their suggestions. Suggest meeting later so they have time to think things through. Give them specific procedures to follow or encourage them to develop their own.

- **Detailed**
  Focus on the task. Give details of procedures and performance standards to meet. Encourage them to make improvements. Give them time to explain in detail. Ask questions. Set deadlines and encourage them not to get bogged down in detail.

You will be more successful in communicating with others if you try to meet their communication needs rather than expecting them to adjust to yours.

Remember, you can't change other people, but you can change yourself. You will be more successful in communicating with others if you try to meet their communication needs rather than expecting them to adjust to yours. In Chapter 2, we discussed talking with your employees to share expectations of each other. At the same time, it would be worthwhile to ask them how they like to be communicated with and to tell them what your preferences are.

Recognize that your employees, coworkers, and managers express themselves much differently than you do. Think of those people with whom you have difficulty working. Do they use words you find bothersome? What are their voice characteristics? What kind of body language do they use when they speak? What is their personality type? Do they send mixed signals?

Take a Moment

Differences in communication can set up barriers between you and your employees that make your jobs harder. Take some time now to identify those barriers and what you can do to change them. For example: "Bob seems to be more of a Social type. I need to show more friendliness by smiling, nodding, taking more time to talk, slowing my speech, and speaking more softly. Also, I need to stop interrupting

Continued on next page

Take a Moment *(continued)*

him and not fold my arms when he is speaking to me. Finally, I need to get his agreement on work deadlines."

____

____

____

____

____

Communication skills are necessary in many aspects of supervision, from face-to-face discussions to phone calls to meetings. Using these skills and knowing how to conduct effective meetings are important demonstrations of higher-level supervisory performance.

Conducting Effective Meetings

Ineffective meetings are the number one complaint in most organizations.

Ineffective meetings are the number one complaint in most organizations. It seems that there are always too many that run too long and get too little done. However, following just a few guidelines can make a positive difference:

1. **Hold only those meetings that are necessary to communicate to all parties involved.** If there is another way to convey the information reliably, such as a memo, e-mail, or conference call, use it instead. If regular meetings are held (weekly, biweekly, etc.), set a goal to complete them in 25 to 40 percent less time.

2. **Always have an agenda.** This is nothing more than a plan that lists topics to be covered and time allotted for each. Distribute it one or two days before the meeting as a reminder for attendees to come prepared. In the meeting, discussions of topics not on the agenda should be delayed until the end or be put on the next meeting's agenda.

3. **Lead assertively.** The meeting leader sets the tone and expectations and is responsible for how well meetings go. However, it is helpful to get participant input and establish rules of conduct, such as "Start on time, end on time," "No side conversations," etc. Also, rotate responsibility for leading meetings among team members. This is an excellent development experience for them. You may need to coach them so that they can be successful.

4. **Send meeting minutes out within 24 hours.** This helps emphasize their importance and reminds meeting attendees of work they need to do.

Communication skills are one of the most important skill sets in supervision.

Communication skills are one of the most important skill sets in supervision. They form the basis for success in many other areas, such as conducting meetings, coaching, counseling, and discipline. Although everyone communicates virtually all of the time, it is not something we ever truly master. It requires constant attention and effort in order to keep developing.

Chapter Summary

We have just considered five key aspects of communication:

1. **Listening**—Always try to understand the other person's position before asking him or her to understand yours.

2. **Word choice**—Avoid using words that can provoke a negative reaction and stop communication.

3. **Tone of voice**—The pitch, volume, quality, and rate of your speech should match the words you are using.

4. **Body language**—The way you look to others also sends a message; your gestures, facial expressions, and posture should support your verbal message and encourage open communication.

5. **Communication style**—Try to adjust your communication style to match the other person's personality type. If they prefer messages to be brief and to the point, you will communicate more effectively with them if you plan your message this way.

Self-Check: Chapter 3 Review

Answers to the following questions appear on pages 121 and 122.

1. Match the terms below with their definitions.

    ____ Hearing

    ____ Listening

    a. Actively trying to understand what the other person is saying.

    b. The physical process that occurs when sound waves vibrate against our eardrums.

2. Which of the following terms is not considered a problem term?

    a. Should
    b. Could or would
    c. Always or never

3. Communicating effectively means using your tone of voice

    to ______________________________ your verbal message.

4. Leaning toward another person sends what message?

    ____

5. Relaxed arms and open hands send what message?

    ____

6. Match the communication techniques below with the personality types that prefer them.

 _____ Forceful
 _____ Social
 _____ Steady
 _____ Detailed

 a. Smile and show that you are friendly. Keep your statements brief and don't go into unnecessary details.
 b. Smile and show that your are friendly. Give details and ask for suggestions.
 c. Come to the point quickly and be brief. Offer alternatives on how to complete a task quickly.
 d. Focus on the task. Give details on procedures and performance standards.

7. List the four guidelines for conducting effective meetings.

 a. ____

 b. ____

 c. ____

 d. ____

Chapter *Four*

Solving Problems and Making Decisions

Chapter Objectives

- ▶ Know how to gather information.
- ▶ Develop and evaluate alternatives.
- ▶ Consider nonmeasurable issues.
- ▶ Select the best alternative.
- ▶ Follow-up effectively.

Dagne didn't know what to do. Her team had been asked to come up with an inexpensive solution to the company's lack of storage space. Just about everyone had an idea, but how could they decide which one was the best?

Problem solving and decision making begin with a challenge to your team or work group that requires a solution.

Problem solving and decision making begin with a challenge to your team or work group that requires a solution. Your job is to address the issue as positively and productively as possible.

Many problems are minor and easily addressed. However, the new supervisor should be cautious and not assume that the solution to a problem is as easy as it looks. Often, quick decisions create other problems—some of which may be worse than the original. The same can be true for decisions that are delayed too long.

Your problem-solving process will run more smoothly, and your final decisions will be more effective, if you follow these four steps:

1. Gather information.
2. Develop and evaluate alternatives.
3. Select the best alternative.
4. Follow up.

Gathering Information

The first step in the problem-solving process is to get a clear understanding of the problem. Start by listing all of the questions about the situation you need to have answered. Here are a few thought starters:

- What will happen if you don't act? What could you gain if you do?
- Who does this situation affect directly and indirectly?
- When did this situation first become apparent? Did it exist before then?
- Are there any deadlines that need to be considered? Can they be extended?
- What are the apparent causes of the problem?
- Is this situation a symptom of some greater problem?

The first step in the problem-solving process is to get a clear understanding of the problem.

Keep asking questions that start with *Who, What, Where, When, Why* and *How* until you are reasonably certain that you understand the nature, size, and effects of the problem. Then summarize the problem in a few sentences. This will help you keep a clear understanding of the problem in your mind and be able to describe it to others. Then, it is time to gather more information.

This can be difficult for many supervisors. Some don't gather enough (this is often true of Forceful and Social personality styles). Others gather too much (this is often true of Steady and Detailed personality styles). Either approach can generate greater problems.

Try to gather 70 to 80 percent of the available information before making a decision.

Few situations readily provide enough information to make us feel completely comfortable with a course of action. However, gathering 100 percent of all available information about a problem is often impractical. Gathering less than 50 percent of the available information can be too risky. A good mental target is to gather what your best estimate tells you is 70 to 80 percent of the available information before proceeding. This judgment will vary by individual and by the situation. However, it is a good guideline to help you avoid moving either too rapidly or too slowly. Here are three primary areas from which you can gather information:

- **People closest to the problem**
  Those who work with the situation and would be most affected by the solution or decision should be involved, first, because of the information they have, and second, because they will be more likely to support a solution if they have input into it. Focus on facts and then let them express their opinions and possible solutions. Be supportive, but stay uncommitted so they won't later feel betrayed if the solution or decision is not what they would like.

- **Experts**
  This refers to anyone who is not directly involved but has credible, relevant information to offer. This may be internal staff, such as Accounting or Human Resources, or outside experts, such as CPAs, attorneys, consultants, or other professionals. Also, talk with your manager, friends within your organization, or counterparts in other organizations who may have faced a similar situation.

- **Personal research**
  Time spent reviewing relevant books, periodicals, and the Internet can be very useful in acquiring current information.

Take a Moment

Consider the last significant problem you faced. Do you feel that you gathered enough information before you made a decision, or did you possibly move too quickly or wait too long? How could you have done a better job in gathering information? Write your observations below.

____

____

____

____

As you face new problems, be aware of your tendencies either to move too quickly or to delay too long and compensate for them. You can do this by continually self-checking against the 70 to 80 percent guideline, by using personal deadlines, and by involving others who have tendencies opposite of yours. This last option can sometimes be frustrating, but it can also help tremendously in improving the quality and timeliness of your decisions.

Gathering information can be tedious, but it is the basis for good decisions. The next step of developing alternatives is equally important, and it requires an equal commitment of time and thought.

Developing and Evaluating Alternatives

A common action that can sometimes be a mistake is to quickly focus on one option as the obvious or best solution and then give little attention to other alternatives. There are three ways to make sure that this one solution really is the best (and to avoid embarrassment if it is not):

1. **List all the reasons against it.**
   Think of someone who might disagree with it and then actively argue against it from his or her point of view.

2. **Brainstorm other options.**
   This is also a good technique when one solution does not stand out as the best. Involve others in the brainstorming to generate as many ideas as possible. Then weigh the pluses and minuses of each.

   When brainstorming, be creative and challenge conventional wisdom or long-held practices. For example, if your problem is in recruiting enough qualified people, perhaps looking at flex-time, part-time, shared work, seniors, providing transportation, or home-based employees can open up whole new groups of prospective employees with good qualifications.

When brain-storming, be creative and challenge conventional wisdom or long-held practices.

3. **Ask *Why?* at least five times for each possible cause of the problem.**
   This will enable you to dig down to the root causes of the problem. Addressing these will result in better solutions.

■ **Example:** If the problem is high turnover, the first cause we might list is:

"We don't hire qualified people to start with."
Why? (1)

"Because interviewers don't do a good job of asking questions about qualifications."
Why? (2)

"Because they don't know how or they feel pressure to get people hired."
Why? (3)

"Because the need for people is so great."
Why? (4)

"Because people are frustrated by the pressure and the lack of training, so they leave."
Why? (5)

"Because supervisors have heavy workloads and many priorities, so they can't train."

The initial reason given for the problem appears to be a poor job of recruiting and interviewing. However, as we go further, deeper causes for the problem appear, such as inadequate planning and training. Continuing to ask *why* beyond this point may highlight more underlying causes. The point is that if we stop at step one or two, the solutions we develop will not solve the problem.

Take a Moment

Consider one of the problems you currently face that seems to keep occurring. Try using all three of the techniques mentioned earlier to find different options aimed more at root causes.

____

____

____

____

Many problems and causes are easy to see or quantify, such as turnover rates, accidents, and costs. However, there are other factors that are harder to measure that you need to consider.

Nonmeasurable Issues

Some issues that affect problem solving and decision making can't be measured.

Some issues that affect problem solving and decision making can't be measured. Yet they can be equally important to the process. Here are a few you should consider along with suggestions for what you can do:

- **Organizational culture**
  Every organization has its own way of acting, talking, and operating. It's important to adapt your actions so that they fit your organization's culture well. For example, your organization may prize a positive attitude, action, and a can-do spirit. If so, phrase your suggestions in that way. Refer to *challenges* or *opportunities,* not *problems.* Use phrases like "attacking the challenge" instead of "addressing the issue."

- **Politics**
  Every organization has them. Your responsibility is to know who the people with influence are and consider your proposed solutions or decisions from their viewpoint. Then follow your manager's advice in making appropriate adjustments.

- **Economic climate**
  Organizations that are doing well financially are generally more open to trying new things and spending money to solve problems. Often, the opposite is true for organizations in which the finances are tight. In this situation, if your proposed actions require the outlay of money, be prepared to offer ways they can be scaled back, completed in smaller parts, or delayed until a later time.

At this point in the process, we have been very thorough in gathering information, developing alternatives, and considering the more intangible issues that could affect our decision. Now it is time to choose the best approach.

Selecting the Best Alternative

If no one option is distinctly better than the others, consider testing two or more approaches at the same time.

Many times the best one or two alternatives stand out after this kind of analysis. However, sometimes no one option is distinctly better than the others. If this is the case, consider testing two or more approaches at the same time. Or you might prioritize the top several options and implement them in order of priority. If you must pick just one option, and it's a difficult choice to make, here are three suggestions that you can try separately or together to help you arrive at the best decision:

1. **Choose the most logical approach.** Then consider the non-measurable issues and make appropriate adjustments. Take no action for 24 hours, and ask yourself if your choice seems like the right course of action. If it doesn't, identify specifically why not and what you might change to make it right.

2. **Consult with people you trust and get their reaction.**

3. **Write down the key reasons why this is the best solution or decision.** Then review these reasons as if you were a third party—like an expert or a judge. How would that person react? Writing the reasons down will also help remind you later of why you made that decision if others argue strongly against it or unforeseen problems develop.

Write down the key reasons why one solution is best, then review the reasons as if you were a third party.

At this point, it is time to act! You have given the issue your best effort and to delay any further would be counterproductive. Believe in yourself and proceed. If for some reason your decision does not work well, you will at least know it was well considered and can use the experience to help in future problem-solving and decision-making challenges.

Take a Moment

Review the suggestions in this section and choose the one(s) that seem to fit you best. Put a check mark by them and write down how you might use them in current or upcoming situations.

____

____

____

____

The problem-solving process can be challenging, especially when there is pressure to find a solution quickly and move on. Making a commitment to follow a good process when the problem is significant pays off with good, long-lasting solutions. The last step to make sure that problems stay solved is following up.

Following Up

One of the best ways to demonstrate a higher level of supervisory responsibility is by following up to see how well your decisions work, as illustrated by the following example:

- Joe manages a warehouse. For several months, he had received reports of a high number of errors in orders shipped from the warehouse, so he implemented a system of double-checking before boxes were sealed and shipped.

  After having his staff try the new procedure for 30 days, he followed up to see if shipping errors had been reduced. He also asked his staff how they felt about the changes and invited them to share other ideas or suggestions. He checked back several more times over the next few months to show his continued interest. The number of errors in shipping were reduced.

Too often, a lack of follow-up allows problems to reoccur.

Joe's actions in the previous example illustrate how to keep problems solved. Too often, a lack of follow-up allows problems to reoccur. In the case of the warehouse, if Joe had not continued to follow up on a regular basis, his staff might have gone back to the old (and perhaps easier) way of doing things. If Joe had assumed that the initial change would "fix" the problem forever, he might be puzzled if the errors started reappearing. His follow-up prevented that.

Chapter Summary

You can make your problem solving more effective and more efficient by following an easy four-step process. Begin by gathering an adequate amount of information from three key sources. Then develop and evaluate possible solutions, avoiding the selection of the first "obvious" alternative.

Next, consider nonmeasurable issues that may affect the decision. Then, make what you consider to be the best choice based on the information you have gathered. Finally, follow up to see how well your solution works over time.

Self-Check: Chapter 4 Review

Answers to these questions appear on page 122.

1. When gathering information about a problem, ask questions

   that begin with ________________, ________________,

   ________________, ________________, ________________,

   and ______________.

2. What are three primary areas from which you can gather information when researching a problem?

   a. ____

   b. ____

   c. ____

3. List three techniques that will help you avoid selecting a solution without considering other alternatives.

   a. ____

   b. ____

   c. ____

4. What are the three nonmeasurable issues to consider before selecting your course of action?

   a. ____

   b. ____

   c. ____

5. After you have selected the best alternative, what is the last step needed to ensure a problem stays solved?

   ____

Chapter *Five*

Managing Conflict

Chapter Objectives

- ▶ Understand why conflict develops and why it's important to address conflict quickly.
- ▶ Manage conflict with peers.
- ▶ Manage conflict with former peers who are now your subordinates.
- ▶ Manage conflict between your subordinates.

Think of the last time you came into conflict with another person. What caused it? Was it because he or she was being stubborn, irrational, or narrow-minded? Often, this is how we view things. We tend to blame others for the conflict and attribute negative reasons to their behavior. We seldom stop to think that the other person might be thinking the same things about us!

Conflict is a normal part of life and business, and it can actually be helpful in stimulating positive change.

Conflict is a normal part of life and business, and it can actually be helpful in stimulating positive change. However, it also can be destructive if it continues over the same issues or is severe.

Why Conflicts Happen

We can gain an advantage in working with others and resolve problems more quickly and effectively by understanding that conflict is generated primarily by differences in three areas:

- Personality type
- Perceptions
- Goals

Let's take a look at each of these in more detail.

Managing Conflict Based on Personality Type

In Chapter 2, four general personality types were defined. Although each of us is a unique mix of all four styles, we tend have one predominant style that we use most of the time. Each style has its own set of needs, and sometimes these conflict with the needs of others, as we can see in the following example:

- Gary has a Forceful personality type. His need for control and directness sometimes causes him to interrupt others, hurry conversations, bark out orders without explanation, and be overly blunt. These behaviors can cause conflicts with other personality types:

    - Social people want to talk and have positive interaction with others. They can become frustrated when they aren't allowed to express themselves and may feel that the Forceful person is being insensitive and rude.

    - Steady people want to accommodate others and avoid abrupt changes. They may be caught off guard and feel intimidated and pushed around by the Forceful person's manner.

    - Detailed people want specifics, time to think things through logically, and a high-quality result. They may feel rushed and think the Forceful person has not given an issue enough thought and does not care about doing things the right way.

Each personality type can have problems with other types simply because they have conflicting needs and methods. Your challenge as a supervisor is to be aware of employees' differing types, adapt to them, and help them adapt to each other. You can do this by helping employees recognize their own types and how they differ from each other and introducing them to some of the communication skills discussed in Chapter 4.

Each personality type can have problems with other types simply because they have conflicting needs and methods.

Take a Moment

Think of another person with whom you have had conflicts in the past. Can you identify that person's personality type? Are there things you could do to adapt to that personality type that would reduce the conflict? List them below.

____

____

____

____

Managing Conflict Based on Perception

We have all heard that no two people see things in the same way. The truth of this statement is apparent when we consider the two main types of factors involved in how people perceive the world:

Both physical and mental factors affect how people perceive the world.

- **Physical factors**
  All of us receive our information about the world through our five senses and interact with the world through our physical abilities. Everything from our eyesight and hearing to our physical skills, health, and disabilities affects how we perceive things. Each person has a unique set of physical circumstances, and this gives her or him a unique perception of the environment.

- **Mental factors**
  There are many factors that act as filters or interpreters of the data we receive through our physical senses. These factors give each person a unique way to focus on and understand the information he or she receives. This is why two people can look at the same data and draw two completely different conclusions.

Here are some examples of mental factors:

- Culture
- Education
- Attitudes
- Values
- Life experience
- Emotional maturity
- Self-esteem
- Intelligence
- Marital status
- Having children
- Religious beliefs
- Gender

It is no wonder that people see things differently and that their views will often conflict.

Although you cannot allow physical and mental factors to serve as excuses for unacceptable behavior, you can consider how they affect employees and coworkers, make accommodations when possible, and identify specific behaviors that you and the other people involved can change to resolve the conflict.

Take a Moment

Can you identify physical or mental factors that affect your own perception? Have they ever been the cause of conflict between you and others? What are some things you could do to deal with these conflicts?

____

____

____

____

Managing Conflict Based on Goals

People in organizations frequently strive to advance by seeking better positions, more resources, and greater influence. Unfortunately, there is never enough of these things to satisfy everyone. This inevitably leads to competition between individuals. Competition can be productive if it motivates people to improve their performance. However, too much competition can lead to conflict in which coworkers view each other as opponents or threats to their personal goals.

Too much competition can lead to conflict in which coworkers view each other as opponents or threats to their personal goals.

People who view each other as threats often act in inappropriate ways and refuse to cooperate with team members.

People who view each other as threats often act in inappropriate ways and refuse to cooperate with team members. This can create a cycle of counter-productive behavior that hinders the effectiveness of the organization. As a supervisor, you need to address this type of conflict before it escalates, or else you could find yourself with an increasing number of problems with productivity, morale, and turnover.

When faced with this type of conflict, you need to remind those involved that their individual goals can be met only when they work together to meet organizational goals. Stress the need for coworkers to view each other as team members first and competitors second. Encourage those in conflict to put petty differences behind them and strive for cooperation in the future.

Take a Moment

Has competition become a source of conflict within your team or work group? What can you do to encourage people to put their differences behind them and work together to meet organizational goals?

____

____

____

____

Handling Common Conflict Situations

Your ability to avoid conflict or to resolve it when it occurs will give you a strong advantage in working with others and in achieving your career goals. Let's see how to deal effectively with conflict in three common situations:

- Conflict with peers
- Conflict with subordinates who used to be coworkers
- Conflict between subordinates

Handling Conflict with Your Peers

When you are in conflict with a peer, keep control of your anger and analyze why the conflict is occurring. Is it because of differences in personality type or perception, or is it due to conflicting goals? Both of these may play a role; however, conflict between peers is often the result of goal conflict and competition. To handle this type of situation, follow these five steps:

Conflict between peers is often the result of goal conflict and competition.

1. **Ask yourself two questions, "How does that person threaten me or my goals?" and "How do I threaten that person?"** If you are not sure about the answers, try asking the other person directly with questions, such as:

   - In what areas do you feel that I am interfering with your goals?
   - What was your purpose when you said those negative comments about my performance to our supervisor?

   The other person may not answer forthrightly at first, so keep probing with specific questions in a nonaggressive way. If you can identify the threats each party poses to the other, you can discuss ways to minimize them. Sometimes, just the fact that you have confronted the other person with the problem behavior will cause her or him to reduce or eliminate it.

2. **Suggest that you set mutual goals.** Look at quality, productivity, safety, and other areas where you both can agree that improvement would be mutually advantageous. Try to find areas where you can work together.

3. **Find ways to help the other person.** This is something for which he or she will probably be grateful. If not, you can at least point to your actions as demonstrations of your good-faith efforts.

4. **Share your expectations of the other person and ask about his or her expectations of you.** For example, if the other person has failed to meet deadlines in getting information to you, you might say, "If you are not able to get the information to me on time, I would appreciate hearing

about it as soon as possible so I can adjust my schedule. Also, I would like to discuss the deadlines to see if we can make them more realistic from your standpoint."

5. **Agree on how you will handle problems between the two of you before they occur.** For example, you might say, "If problems develop in the future, let's agree that you and I will meet within 24 hours of the situation to discuss immediate solutions and ways to prevent that problem from reoccurring."

Take a Moment

Consider the last time you had a conflict with a peer. What factors do you think contributed to it? What might you have done differently to resolve the conflict more positively? Write your answers below.

____

____

____

____

Handling Conflict with Subordinates Who Were Once Peers

■ Monique dreaded her next meeting with Wayne. She always thought the two of worked well together when they were coworkers. But since she'd been promoted to supervisor, they couldn't seem to agree on anything.

Supervising people who were once your coworkers can be one of the new supervisor's greatest challenges.

Supervising people who were once your coworkers can be one of the new supervisor's greatest challenges. There are several reasons for this:

- Former coworkers have been used to talking freely with you about issues ranging from pay to work rules to the wisdom of management. Now they may wonder if they can be as open with you and may believe that you have become more guarded and distant from them.

- Some former coworkers may feel that they have the same—or better—qualifications as you and are jealous or disappointed that they were passed over. This can be exacerbated by their perceptions of your weaknesses, which can be blown out of proportion.

- Minor conflicts between you and a former coworker could now be seen as causes for greater resentment and fear since you are now in a position of greater power.

Following these five steps can help you deal with this awkwardness:

1. **Talk with the person(s) with whom you are having conflict.** Ask them directly why they have problems with you. Are they jealous, disappointed, or threatened? Avoid any appearance of threat, and keep probing nonaggressively.

2. **Express your understanding of their feelings.** Say something like "I'd feel the same if I were in your place."

3. **Minimize your position of having power over them.** Use phrases like "working together" or "working with you," and ask for their help in doing things. Don't worry about appearing weak. You have all the power you need and can use it at a later time if necessary.

4. **Ask for their opinions about changes that can be made.** Everyone likes to be asked his or her opinion. Make sure you follow up by expressing your appreciation and giving feedback about whether ideas can be used.

5. **Counsel with them about changing specific behaviors.** If a former coworker refuses to work with you to reduce the conflict, then you will have to begin the counseling and discipline process. Remember that you have tried to work with him or her to resolve the problems. If that person doesn't respond, it is his or her choice.

Take a Moment

If you have had this kind of conflict, which of the five steps mentioned earlier would have worked best to help resolve the problem? Take a moment now and write down your ideas about what you might have done then and could do in the future with that person.

____

____

____

____

Handling Conflict Between Subordinates

Act quickly to resolve conflicts between subordinates.

Supervisors are often reluctant to intervene between warring subordinates because they believe that as adults, they should be able to work things out themselves. But in reality, that seldom happens—the conflict simply gets worse. Instead of allowing this to happen, you should act quickly to resolve the conflict. If you don't, there are two negative consequences:

- The conflict could hurt the productivity and morale of your department, and that can affect how you are regarded by *your* supervisor.

- Your credibility with your other employees could be hurt. They will resent the fact that you are allowing the conflict to continue and cause their work lives to be unpleasant.

Here are four steps to take when you are confronted with this situation:

1. **Document the problem behavior.** This will allow you to cite specifics when you talk with each party. Also, if you eventually must begin the discipline process with anyone, you already have the necessary records.

2. **Meet with each person individually.** Ask each for her or his view of the problem—how it started, what the issues are, etc. Each person will see the other person as the problem, so keep probing until you have a complete understanding of each viewpoint. Look to see how much of the conflict is based in differences in personality styles, differences in perception, or in competition. If the conflict is minor, offer counseling about these issues and clearly state that you want the conflict stopped. Also, give clear instructions about the behavior you want to see changed and the consequences if it is not.

   If the conflict continues or shows up in other ways, go on to Step 3.

Give clear instructions about the behavior you want to see changed and the consequences if it is not.

3. **Meet with the conflicting parties together.** Open the meeting by giving them the ground rules:

   - This is a problem-solving meeting, not a court of law. There is no guilt to be assigned, only solutions to be found.

   - You, the supervisor, will state each party's position first and will then let him or her clarify it. No one can speak until both positions are expressed. Discussion will focus only on solutions. Interrupting is not allowed.

   - Each person's feelings and perceptions are facts to them and will be addressed as such.

   - All solutions will be mutually agreed upon by both parties with the goal of seeking win-win outcomes. If that is not possible, you may impose solutions which one or both parties may not like. If the conflict continues, both parties will be subject to the disciplinary process.

4. **Follow up once or twice with each person.** Don't assume that one meeting will make the conflict disappear. If the employees see that you are serious by your continued interest, they will be more likely to try to avoid problems.

Dealing with conflict is one of the more unpleasant challenges of supervision—and life. Many supervisors tend to ignore conflict or just tolerate it. Unfortunately, conflict almost never gets better on its own; in fact, it often gets worse. Analyzing the causes and taking positive action can help minimize conflict and sometimes eliminate it. It is not uncommon for people who have resolved their differences to become allies and even friends. Resolving conflict is a unique skill that can help improve the quality of your life and your opportunity to advance.

Chapter Summary

We can identify three main reasons why conflict occurs:

- Differences in personality types
- Differences in perception
- Differences in goals

Each of these types of conflict can be managed effectively if those involved take the time to discuss their differences, adapt to each other, and remember that their primary responsibility is to work together to meet the goals of the organization.

Supervisors generally face three common conflict situations:

- Conflict with peers
- Conflict with subordinates who were once coworkers
- Conflict between subordinates

Rather than avoiding conflict in the hope that it will resolve on its own, supervisors can handle each of these conflict situations by following a series of steps that include nonaggressively probing for information about what is causing the conflict and working together with those involved to deal with specific issues.

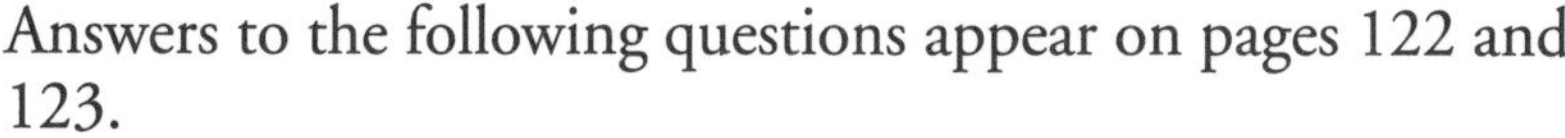

Self-Check: Chapter 5 Review

Answers to the following questions appear on pages 122 and 123.

1. Why might a Forceful personality type create conflict when dealing with a Social personality type?

   ____

   ____

   ____

2. What are the two main factors that can cause people to perceive information differently?

   a. ____

   b. ____

3. What is the main cause of conflict with peers?

   ____

4. What are two questions you should ask yourself during the first step of resolving conflict with a peer?

   a. ____

   b. ____

5. What are the two reasons you need to act quickly when conflict develops between two of your subordinates?

   a. ____

   b. ____

Chapter *Six*

Enacting Progressive Discipline

Chapter Objectives

- ▶ Understand the purpose of discipline.
- ▶ Know the three keys to effective discipline.
- ▶ Turn progressive discipline into positive discipline.
- ▶ Know what to say to employees during the discipline process.

Many people think of discipline as a negative process—one that is based on punishing the employee for problem behavior. This type of attitude can create feelings of anxiety and fear for both the supervisor and the employee. However, the discipline process can be an opportunity to turn a problem situation into one in which everyone wins—the employee, the supervisor, and the organization. Here are two important elements that can help you turn discipline into a positive process:

- Understand that the purpose of discipline is to change behavior—not to punish. In fact, the Latin root word for discipline is *discere* which means "to learn." The supervisor's role is to help the employee learn how to behave appropriately—not to be a police officer or a judge.

The success of discipline rests mainly with the employee.

- Understand that the success of discipline rests mainly with the employee. The supervisor is responsible for offering choices, training, and encouragement, as well as making the employee aware of the consequences of her or his choices. The employee is responsible for improving performance.

Three Keys to Effective Discipline

Regardless of the steps in your organization's disciplinary process, these three guidelines will help you help your employees to succeed:

- **Be consistent and fair.** *Consistency* means treating all employees the same in similar circumstances. *Fairness* means balancing the employee's personal circumstances with the standard of consistency, as in the following example:

  - LaVonne has no record of tardiness over several years, but then she is tardy several times in quick succession due to a difficult personal problem. She may warrant a little more time to correct the problem than Sherman, who has been chronically late over the last six months and given many weak excuses. However, LaVonne must still correct her tardiness just as Sherman must.

Be consistent and fair with all your employees.

- **Don't wait to see if things improve.** The earlier you address problems, the more likely you and the employee will be successful.

- **Document specific problem behavior.** This is critically important, and it is the area in which most supervisors are weakest. Focusing your efforts on documentation will give you two great advantages:

  - It allows you to be specific in talking with employees, which can generate more positive responses. For example, saying to an employee, "I've noticed your attitude has slipped this past week," could provoke a negative response. Instead, try saying, "I noticed you were late two days last week and that you were sarcastic in speaking to Bob yesterday. Neither of these things is like you. What caused the problems?" This is more likely to get a positive response.

  - It provides the written evidence your organization might need to defend against union or legal challenges to disciplinary actions.

When documenting, avoid making judgments or using negative generalities. Instead, focus on specific employee behaviors—not personality or attitude. Describe what you see and hear. Compare these two different ways of documenting:

Too General/Judgmental	Descriptive
• Jim has developed a bad attitude.	• In the last week, Jim has been 10 minutes late three times; he does not make eye contact when addressed and either does not answer or speaks in a harsh or sarcastic tone.
• Janet is insecure and difficult.	• On this date, Janet argued with Pat and Brent about operational issues she isn't responsible for and loudly told Bob in front of a customer, "You're really stupid! I'm not getting fired because of you!"

Always document employee problems when you first notice them, whether or not you are considering the discipline process.

Always document employee problems when you first notice them, whether or not you are considering the discipline process. That way, if you do decide to begin the discipline process, your documentation will be ready. Waiting to document can delay the process.

Documenting need not take a long time. Just answer these questions briefly, specifically, and descriptively:

- *Who* did it?
- *What* did he or she do or say?
- *When* (date and time) did he or she do or say it?
- *Where* did the incident occur?

Take a Moment

Think of the last time you noticed a problem with an employee. How would you document it using the *who, what, when,* and *where* questions?

____

____

____

____

Good documentation provides a strong foundation as you continue to follow the steps of your discipline process.

Making Progressive Discipline Positive

Most companies have a discipline process with steps that lead to progressively more stringent consequences if an employee does not change his or her behavior. Those steps often follow this model:

First Step: Oral Warning

Second Step: Written Warning

Third Step: Suspension Without Pay

Fourth Step: Termination of Employment

This type of progressive discipline system has been used for decades. Unfortunately, it has often been viewed as a guide for progressively greater punishment. This has contributed to the negative feelings about the discipline process. Following the steps on the next several pages will help you make progressive discipline more positive.

Step 1: Examine Your Own Attitude

As you consider what you should do about an employee who is behaving inappropriately, here are two questions to ask yourself:

1. Is my purpose to:
   A. Correct? or B. Punish?

2. Do I want to:
   A. Solve the problem? or B. Vent my anger?

If you can honestly answer *A* to both questions, you are in a good position to begin the process of discipline positively. If your answer to either question is *B,* then it is to your advantage to wait until your anger has passed or to discuss the situation with your supervisor, a colleague, or Human Resources so you can develop a more positive frame of mind.

Step 2: Use a Checklist to Prepare for Your Meeting

This ensures that you have everything you need to effectively communicate with the employee. Here is a summary of one called FOSA+:

Do you have documented specifics of the problem behavior?

Facts: Do you have documented specifics of the problem behavior? Can you describe its negative effects on the organization or other employees? How, specifically, does it deviate from standards or expectations?

Objectives: What specifically do you want or don't want the employee to do? Providing specifics tells the employee how she or he can succeed.

Solutions: What are the steps the employee needs to take to accomplish the objectives?

Actions: What are the actions you must take (consequences) if the employee does not correct the problem?

±: Are there any extra efforts you can make to help the employee succeed?

This checklist not only helps you be better prepared and more confident before approaching an employee, but also ensures that you have done those things that an outside party (such as a court or a government agency) would look for.

Step 3: Use Positive Language

Start by using positive terms in discussions with employees. For example:

Use positive terms in discussions with employees.

Instead of	Try
• Oral Warning	• Reminder
• Written Warning	• Improvement Plan
• Suspension	• Decision Leave
• Termination	• Leave the Organization

Use of these terms is not meant to make the process seem less serious. Nor does your choice of terms make a difference legally. But positive language does address employees as adults who have the responsibility for changing their own behavior, which helps make the discipline process seem less punitive.

Another powerful way to make progressive discipline more positive is to make the decision leave one or two days of time off *with* pay instead of without pay. You may need permission for this, but consider how it could help salvage an employee who is getting close to losing his or her job and is probably feeling very stressed.

Suspension Without Pay	Decision Leave with Pay
• Lack of pay provokes resentment and shifts the employee's focus from "What should I do differently?" to "Look at the terrible thing they've done to me!"	• Pay underscores the seriousness and positive support and keeps the employee focused on his or her problem.
• Places control and responsibility for the next step with the organization.	• Places control and responsibility for the next step with the employee.

When the employee comes back, have a meeting to discuss whether or not she or he will make the necessary changes. This gives the employee full responsibility for keeping her or his job, reduces the negativity of the process, and may even shorten the duration of the disciplinary process.

Organizations that use paid decision leaves report that there is little or no extra cost involved, and they have greater success helping employees turn their work problems around. Also, employees sometimes make the decision not to return, and that is better than having them return angry from losing pay. Finally, a paid decision leave shows the organization's good-faith effort to help the employee, and that can help if courts or government agencies get involved.

Once you have documentation and a positive plan in place, the next step is to talk with the employee who is having problems.

Begin providing an employee with feedback the moment you notice a performance problem.

Choosing What to Say to Your Employee

You should begin providing an employee with feedback the moment you notice a performance problem, before you start the discipline process. These conversations are informal and private. Your goal is to point out the deviation from standards in a casual, concerned way.

Often, you can start with a friendly question, as in this example:

- "Helen, I've noticed you've missed some deadlines in getting reports done over the past couple of weeks. Is there a problem I can help you with?"

Document your conversation even at this early stage so that if problems continue, you will have a good basis to proceed to the first step of progressive discipline.

Providing the Oral Warning or Reminder

Once an employee gets to the first step of progressive discipline, your discussions should continue to show concern, but be more structured. As with your earlier discussions, they should be documented, though not necessarily signed by the employee. Your goal at this point is to advise the employee that behavior correction is necessary. Stay focused on the issue rather than becoming personal. We can observe the effectiveness of this approach by comparing the following two examples:

Your goal at this point is to advise the employee that behavior correction is necessary.

- "Helen, you're late again with your reports. You really need to stop lagging behind."

- "Helen, the delays in your reports have slowed the work of other people in the department. This needs to be improved right away. What can you do to accomplish this?"

The first example takes a judgmental approach to the problem and could be perceived as blaming, which could provoke a negative response. The second example deals with the same facts, but it presents them in a way that focuses on behavior and asks the employee to help develop a solution.

Take a Moment

Think about a discussion you need to have with an employee with a performance problem. What could you say at the beginning of the conversation to show concern, require change, and focus on the problem behavior—not attitude or personality?

____

____

Developing the Written Warning or Improvement Plan

In this second step, you and the employee will develop a written plan for the employee's improvement, which you both will sign. You should also send a follow-up memo to the employee to confirm the main points of your conversation and what will happen if the employee does not take steps to improve.

Use the FOSA+ checklist as a guide for your conversation; below are some tips for successfully completing each step.

Facts: Use your documentation to describe the behaviors that need to change. Expect that the employee might be defensive and attempt to shift blame or change the subject. Focus the conversation back to the employee's behavior. Listen to his or her side. Document his or her comments.

Objectives: State clearly what you expect.

Solutions: Ask the employee for his or her ideas about changes that can be made. Be open to hearing about changes in procedure, resources, etc., but stay focused on the employee's behavior. Write a plan (better yet, have the employee write it), and be sure both of you sign it.

Actions: Ask the employee for her or his commitment to change. Without apologizing or threatening, state what the next step is if the employee does not choose to change.

±: Ask if you can offer any help, training, or other suggestions that would assist the employee.

Making a Suspension or Decision Leave

Use the FOSA+ guide again for your conversation. In the initial (Facts) step, review the last meeting, the written improvement plan, and the specific problems that have occurred since. Continue to show concern and a willingness to help.

Restate your expectations and advise the employee that he or she is being sent home for a specific amount of time to consider whether he or she will make the necessary changes. Write a brief statement for the employee to sign that describes your conversation and states that failure to change will require the employee to leave the organization.

If you use the Decision Leave approach, advise the employee that the two of you will meet when he or she first comes back. Also advise that in that meeting, he or she will need to sign a statement about what his or her decision is.

If you use the Decision Leave approach, advise the employee that the two of you will meet when he or she first comes back.

Leaving the Organization

The purpose of this conversation is to notify the employee that she or he is no longer employed with your organization. Here are six tips to help you and the employee deal with this situation:

1. **Have a witness.** This helps protect you and the organization against possible untrue accusations in the future, and it may help in inhibiting angry responses from the employee.

2. **Come to the point quickly and be brief.** The longer the meeting lasts, the more difficult it can become.

3. **Act respectfully and sympathetically.** Give the employee a chance to respond, but don't reexplain the process or offer advice. This will not help the employee and may lead you to say something that could later be a problem.

4. **Have answers for probable questions.** This will probably include benefits information, how references will be answered, etc. If you're not sure of an answer, assure the employee that you or a Human Resources representative will get it.

5. **Know what organization property you need to recover and how and when you want the employee to leave.** Plan the meeting and the departure in a way that maintains the employee's dignity and avoids causing problems with his or her transportation.

6. **Rehearse phrases for the opening and the close.** If necessary, read a statement or a letter. Employees will remember what

was said and how it was said, so give this careful attention. Here are some suggestions:

- **Opening the meeting:** "Jim, we've met several times over the past six months concerning your difficulty in complying with our attendance policy. When we met two months ago, I advised you that you would no longer be able to work here if you were absent again within six months. Since you were absent yesterday, we have reached that point. Our meeting today is to tell you that you can no longer be employed here and to discuss what the organization will do to help you in your transition."

- **Response to a request for reconsideration:** "Jim, at this point, that is no longer possible."

- **Response to anger:** "I understand that you're angry, and I am sorry that we've come to this point."

- **Close:** "Would you like more time before we walk to your work area?"

Progressive discipline can be a challenge, but it need not be something to avoid. Using an approach in which the primary responsibility for change is the employee's can make the process much more positive and more likely to succeed.

Chapter Summary

Three guidelines that will help you enact progressive discipline effectively are: be consistent and fair; don't wait to see if things improve; and document specific problem behavior using who, what, when, where, and why questions.

You can make sure the process stays positive by examining your own attitude toward the situation, using a checklist like FOSA+ to help you prepare for your meeting, and using positive language throughout the process. Though each company's disciplinary steps are different, a typical sequence includes oral warning/reminder, written warning/improvement plan, suspension/decision leave, and termination/leaving the organization.

Self-Check: Chapter 6 Review

Answers to these questions appear on page 123.

1. The purpose of discipline is to ____________________

   ____________________, not to ____________________.

2. List three guidelines that are keys to effective discipline.

   a. ____________________
   b. ____________________
   c. ____________________

3. What four questions can help you create detailed documentation of employee behavior?

   a. ____________________
   b. ____________________
   c. ____________________
   d. ____________________

4. What are the three ways to make progressive discipline more positive?

   a. ____________________
   b. ____________________
   c. ____________________

5. What does FOSA+ stand for?

   F ____________________
   O ____________________
   S ____________________
   A ____________________
   \+ ____________________

Chapter *Seven*

Understanding Employment Law

Chapter Objectives

- ▶ Understand your responsibility for complying with employment laws.
- ▶ Know what the major laws are.
- ▶ Recognize sexual harassment and how to prevent it.
- ▶ Know your organization's safety and health responsibilities.
- ▶ Apply the laws in critical parts of the employment process.

With more than 400 federal laws regulating employment and a large number of similar state laws, the job of supervising people and avoiding legal problems can seem overwhelming. However, becoming aware of the major laws and the most common problems to avoid will help you feel more confident about what you should do.

Employment laws apply to every aspect of employment from recruiting to firing.

In general, employment laws apply to every aspect of employment from recruiting to firing. They ensure that no one in the workplace is unfairly treated solely because of membership in a *protected group,* such as race, national origin, gender, pregnancy, religion, age, disability, or military service. A supervisor's responsibility is to ignore his or her own personal bias in any of these areas and treat everyone consistently and fairly on the basis of her or his performance.

Now, let's review several laws that are likely to affect you and your employees.

Reviewing Major Federal Employment Laws

There are numerous federal and state employment laws that might affect you as a supervisor. Here are the major federal laws and a brief explanation of each:

- **The Fair Labor Standards Act of 1938**
  Requires employers to pay at least the hourly minimum wage plus overtime to hourly workers who work more than 40 hours per week.

- **Civil Rights Act of 1964, Title VII**
  Prohibits discrimination on the basis of race, sex, or religion. Resulted in the creation of the Equal Employment Opportunity Commission (EEOC).

- **Occupational Safety and Health Act of 1970**
  Requires safety standards for the workplace. Prohibits the termination of employees who complain about unsafe working conditions.

- **Pregnancy Discrimination Act of 1978**
  Prohibits discrimination on the basis of pregnancy or childbirth.

- **Age Discrimination in Employment Act, amended 1978**
  Prohibits discrimination against persons age 40 and over.

- **Americans with Disabilities Act of 1990**
  Prohibits discrimination against persons with disabilities.

- **Civil Rights Act of 1991**
  Allows former employees who win discrimination lawsuits to receive punitive damages and damages for emotional distress in addition to back pay and attorneys' fees.

- **Family and Medical Leave Act of 1993**
  Provides covered employees up to 12 weeks of unpaid, job-protected leave for certain family and medical reasons.

Not all federal and state laws apply to all businesses. Coverage often depends on the number of people employed. However, it is important to be aware of these laws and to be prepared for situations in which they do apply.

These laws are not intended to compel you to hire or retain unqualified or poorly performing employees. They simply require organizations not to discriminate against people on the basis of personal attributes that do not affect their ability to do the job.

Take a Moment

Which state and federal laws apply to your organization? If your organization has a human resources department, check with an HR specialist to find out. If you have no human resources department, try checking with your state's employment commissions.

Of all of the many legal issues that can affect you and your employees, two have become much more visible in recent years, and it is important to understand both in depth. The first is sexual harassment, and the second is occupational safety.

Preventing Sexual Harassment

Sexual harassment is one of the fastest-growing areas of complaint being lodged with state and federal agencies.

Sexual harassment is considered a form of sexual discrimination. It is one of the fastest-growing areas of complaint being lodged with state and federal agencies. In addition to being illegal, sexual harassment also generates many business problems, such as:

- Decreased productivity
- Decreased morale
- Increased conflict between employees
- Increased workers' compensation claims
- Increased legal fees
- Increased mistakes

- Increased lateness and absenteeism
- Increased sick leave
- Distraction of management
- Negative publicity

Recognizing Sexual Harassment

There are two kinds of sexual harassment:

- **Quid pro quo sexual harassment**
  This occurs when a manager or supervisor:
  - Offers hiring, promotions, etc., in return for the employee's granting of sexual favors.
  - Transfers, disciplines, or fires an employee who refuses to grant sexual favors or who ends a romantic relationship.
- **Hostile environment sexual harassment**
  This occurs when there is verbal or nonverbal behavior in the workplace that:
  - Focuses on a person's sexuality.
  - Is unsolicited or unwelcome and is repeated or severe.
  - Negatively affects an employee's performance.

  Here are some examples of behavior that can create a hostile environment:
  - Off-color jokes, comments about one's sex life, repeated requests for a date
  - Leering, staring too long, making crude gestures
  - Posting or passing around suggestive or pornographic pictures, calendars, etc.
  - Touching, such as brushes, pats, hugs, or shoulder rubs

Supervisors need to understand three key issues related to both types of sexual harassment:

Sexual harassment is based on how the target person perceives the behavior of the other person.

- Sexual harassment is based on how the target person perceives the behavior of the other person, not on the harassing person's intent. Consider the following example:

  - Carolyn hated going out to the service department in the car dealership where she worked. The mechanics were all men, and they liked to display "swimsuit" calendars they received from auto parts manufacturers. The calendars embarrassed Carolyn, but when she complained to her supervisor, she was told that the mechanics didn't mean any harm and she should just ignore them.

  Carolyn's supervisor could be in serious trouble if Carolyn decided to file a sexual harassment claim. Even if employee A claims that he or she was only kidding employee B with jokes, gestures, etc., A's actions could still be defined as sexual harassment if employee B sees the behavior as sexual in nature and offensive.

Anyone in the workplace can sexually harass an employee.

- Anyone in the workplace can sexually harass an employee. This means that inappropriate behavior from managers, supervisors, coworkers, and subordinates can be considered sexual harassment. Sexual harassment can also come from outside the organization, as in the following example:

  - "I wish you'd do something about that buyer from the office supply company," George told his supervisor. "She can say some pretty crude things, and I'm getting tired of it."

    "What can I do about it?" the supervisor responded. "She doesn't even work for us. Besides, she represents one of our biggest clients. You can put up with some crude behavior for the amount of money she spends with us."

  Like the supervisor in our previous example, George's supervisor is making a serious mistake by ignoring this instance of harassment. Vendors, visitors, and clients can also commit sexual harassment in your workplace.

- Supervisors have a responsibility to stop sexual harassment whenever they see it. This means reporting it to management, taking appropriate action, and cooperating in any investigation.

Five Guidelines for Preventing Sexual Harassment

In order to prevent sexual harassment, supervisors can help employees by providing them with these five guidelines:

1. **Limit physical contact.** Offer a handshake rather than a hug or an encouraging word instead of a pat on the back. Maintain an arm's length of distance between each other.

2. **Use the same-sex standard.** Ask yourself if you would say the same thing to someone of the same sex. If not, it might not be appropriate.

3. **Use the family standard.** If the behavior you're directing toward your coworker were directed at one of your family members by someone else, would it be okay with you? If not, then your behavior is probably not appropriate.

4. **Recognize the line between appropriate and inappropriate behavior at work.** Some joking can be fun and can help group cohesiveness. However, it can be difficult to predict how joking about the topic of sex will be perceived in a work environment. It is generally best just to avoid it.

5. **Speak up assertively when someone else's behavior makes you uncomfortable.** Many times this will stop it. If this behavior doesn't stop, complain to your supervisor.

Take a Moment

Does your organization currently offer any training on avoiding sexual harassment? If it does, how long has it been since workers on your team or in your department were trained on this subject? If it doesn't, what can you do to be sure that your employees understand the difference between appropriate and inappropriate behavior?

____

____

____

The subject of sexual harassment can be confusing and controversial. As a supervisor, you need to understand what constitutes sexual harassment and be able to communicate that information to your employees. Another issue you need to understand and be able to discuss with employees is workplace safety. An important responsibility for every supervisor is to make sure that employees leave work as healthy as when they arrived.

Maintaining Occupational Safety

The federal Occupational Safety and Health Act (OSHA) and similar legislation in virtually every state are laws that apply to every private employer, regardless of company size. They require employers to provide a hazard-free workplace or, if hazards are unavoidable, to provide employees with proper information, equipment, and training to protect themselves from harm.

Occupational safety laws have specific requirements in the following areas:

- Hygiene and sanitation
- Noise
- Lighting and room temperature
- Restrooms
- First aid
- Showers (where necessary)
- Smoking
- Fire and electrical safety
- Toxic waste and hazardous chemicals
- Protection from violence

Additional safety regulations cover specific hazardous occupations from metal fabrication to construction to health care.

There are also requirements for reporting accidents and unsafe working conditions. For example, any injury causing a worker to miss more than one week of work is considered serious and must be reported to OSHA within 48 hours of the attending physician's examination.

There are many specific safety provisions for every industry and work environment, including the office. Your responsibility as a supervisor is to be aware of those that apply to your organization and work area. If you have questions about this, contact your supervisor or the human resources department. If you need further information, contact either your state labor agency or OSHA.

Here are three key aspects of OSHA regulations that relate to every work situation:

- Employers must display a poster in the workplace that notifies employees of their OSHA rights.
- If employees complain that a work area is unsafe, the employer must investigate it. Employees cannot be required to put themselves at risk. Also, employees have the right to report safety violations to OSHA, and they are protected from being fired or disciplined for doing so.
- OSHA and state safety inspectors have the right to inspect workplaces without notice periodically and to talk with employees without a supervisor being present.

Ninety percent of all occupational accidents are caused by human error or poor judgment, and this makes workplace safety an issue that all supervisors need to take seriously.

Take a Moment

Are you familiar with the OSHA regulations for your work environment? If not, get information from your human resources department or from your local OSHA office.

Now that we've reviewed some of the most important laws and regulations that can affect your workplace, let's look at how employment laws apply in two critical stages of the employment process—hiring and firing.

Establishing Fair Hiring Practices

As we saw at the beginning of this chapter, a number of federal laws protect employees from discrimination in the workplace. One area in which it is especially important to avoid the appearance of discrimination is the hiring process.

These three guidelines will help keep your hiring process fair and legal:

- Job requirements should focus on what is really necessary to do the job so they don't unintentionally screen out protected groups. For example, at one time, many fire departments had height and weight requirements that unfairly screened out women, Asians, and other groups of people who tend to be of smaller stature. Being a certain height and weight really wasn't necessary to perform the job of firefighter: the primary concern was that firefighters be strong enough to rescue people who might be trapped in a burning building. By changing these physical requirements to performance requirements, such as requiring applicants to be able to lift a certain amount of weight, fire departments could make hiring decisions based on what was necessary to do the job without discriminating.

- Application and interview questions should focus on the applicants' experience and ability to do the job. Never ask questions regarding an applicant's

  - Age
  - Marital status
  - Child-care arrangements
  - Ethnic or religious background

  If you need to determine whether an applicant is available for weekend work or overtime, avoid prying into his or her personal life. Instead, ask "Can you work weekends?" or "Are you available for overtime?"

- If a qualified applicant has a disability, the organization may have to make some accommodations to enable the person to do the job, as long as the cost is not unreasonable.

Once you have hired an employee, you can be reasonably certain that treating him or her fairly and positively in the ways described in this and earlier chapters will help you to avoid most legal problems. However, in the unfortunate event that you have to terminate an employee, you need to pay careful attention to the firing process.

Following Appropriate Firing Guidelines

As a supervisor, you need to consider two key factors at the time of firing:

- Failure to be fair and consistent in enforcing the organization's rules or failure to follow the organization's progressive discipline procedure can provide employees with grounds to file lawsuits for wrongful discharge. They can also file discrimination suits if they are members of protected groups.

- Saying or implying that employees can keep their jobs for as long as they work hard and stay out of trouble can be viewed as a contract. If you later fire them, they may have grounds to sue for breach of contract.

It may seem that there is a lot to remember. However, being aware of these laws and using common sense and a fair, performance-based approach to supervising your employees will help you avoid time-consuming and costly legal problems.

Chapter Summary

A variety of federal and state laws ensure that no one in the workplace is treated unfairly because of membership in a protected group, such as race, national origin, gender, pregnancy, religion, age, disability, or military service.

Sexual harassment has become a frequent legal concern in recent years. Sexual harassment can take the form of quid pro quo sexual harassment or hostile environment sexual harassment.

The federal Occupational Safety and Health Act (OSHA) raises a number of legal concerns relating to employee safety. Employers must maintain a safe workplace for employees and investigate employee reports of any unsafe conditions.

The hiring and firing processes also raise a number of legal concerns. Be sure you follow all legal and company procedures whenever you hire or fire an employee.

Self-Check: Chapter 7 Review

Answers to the following questions appear on pages 123 and 124.

1. What is covered by the Civil Rights Act of 1964, Title VII?

 ____

 ____

 ____

2. What are the two types of sexual harassment?

 a. ______________________________

 b. ______________________________

3. Which of the following is not a guideline for preventing sexual harassment?

 a. Limit physical contact.
 b. Quietly ignore behavior that makes you uncomfortable.
 c. Use the family standard.

4. Which of the following is not a key aspect of OSHA regulations that affect every work situation?

 a. Employers must display a poster in the workplace that notifies employees of their OSHA rights.

 b. If employees complain that a work area is unsafe, the employer must investigate it.

 c. OSHA and state safety inspectors can inspect workplaces if they provide employers with one day's notice and can talk with employees as long as a supervisor is present.

5. To avoid discriminating against job applicants, job application and interview questions should focus on

____

6. What could happen if you fail to be fair and consistent in enforcing your organization's rules or fail to follow the organization's progressive discipline procedure when firing an employee?

____

____

Chapter *Eight*

Managing Your Time and Stress

Chapter Objectives

- ▶ Master the three keys to managing your time.
- ▶ Recognize why, when, and how to delegate.
- ▶ Explain the positives and negatives of stress.
- ▶ Develop an action plan to make stress work for you.

When we refer to time management, we are actually talking about managing our own actions. Like many other parts of business and life, this requires planning and doing a few things differently. The reward is increased control of our lives and greater achievement of our goals.

Three key elements can help you make the most of your time:

- ◆ Organize your work.
- ◆ Prioritize your tasks.
- ◆ Minimize unproductive activities.

Let's look at each of these and see what you can do in each area.

Efficiency experts estimate that the average person wastes up to one hour a day looking for papers, files, phone numbers, etc.

Getting Organized

Efficiency experts estimate that the average person wastes up to one hour a day looking for papers, files, phone numbers, etc. This is largely caused by clutter. Many people have a cluttered work area and say that they know where everything is. However, studies have shown that reducing clutter helps nearly everyone work more efficiently.

The main reason people keep papers, files, and books stacked in piles on their desks and throughout their offices is to remind them of projects they have to do. Unfortunately, this works too well. Whenever they look up, they are distracted by the projects confronting them and their train of thought is interrupted. Any interruption, whether it's a visitor, a phone call, or an unfinished task, hurts work efficiency in three ways:

- The interruption itself takes time away from the task at hand.
- After the interruption, it takes time to refocus on the original task.
- Frequent interruptions that force one to stop and start a project over and over reduce the quality of work.

Even if each distraction takes just a few seconds, when they are multiplied by the number of times they occur, they take a significant toll in lost time and reduced quality of work. With this in mind, let's look at two ways to get organized that will make a big difference in reducing distractions:

- Getting rid of clutter
- Scheduling your tasks

Getting Rid of Clutter

Removing clutter can be a challenge, so approach it in several small steps:

1. **Clean out files in cabinets and your desk.**
   Throw away anything more than one year old unless legal requirements or good judgment says to keep it. Studies indicate that we will never use up to 60 percent of what we have kept. A good guideline is, "If in doubt, pitch it out."

   Tip: Clean out the files in the hard drive of your computer in the same way.

2. **Clear your desktop.**

   - Throw away or file old reading, such as newspapers more than one week old and magazines and memos more than one month old.

Studies indicate that we will never use up to 60 percent of what we have kept.

- Write down all of the tasks you have to do (including those stacked on your desk and throughout your work area) on a sheet of paper. This will become your Master List, and it ensures that you will not forget any task. We will use it later to prioritize tasks.

- Place all the papers and files on your desk into your newly purged file drawers. Those projects that are too thick to put into drawers should be stacked so that they are out of your line of sight when you are working.

Take a Moment

Look around your work area. How long has it been since you cleaned out files, threw away old reading material, and reorganized your current projects? If it's been a while, schedule a block of time to do it now.

3. **Set up an orderly flow of work into and out of your office.** Divide all incoming work into the following categories:

   - **To do this week.** Write these tasks on your Master List and keep related papers in a to-do file folder. This is the one folder you should keep on top of your desk.

   - **To do in coming weeks or to file for future reference.** Write these tasks on your Master List and keep related papers in files in your desk. Make notes on your calendar or place the time-sensitive papers in dated files.

   - **To read.** Newspapers, journals, etc., should be set aside for designated 10-minute reading periods several times each week.

Scheduling Your Tasks

Designate certain times of the day to work on specific tasks. Do your hardest tasks at the time of day when you are at your best. For example:

Do your hardest tasks at the time of day when you are at your best.

- Deidre had a major project that she needed to complete. She'd tried to work on it for several days, but it seemed that interruptions and smaller tasks kept getting in the way. By the time she got around to her project, it was late in the afternoon and her energy was running low. She decided to reschedule her time so that she could have two hours in the morning when her energy was highest to work on her project. Her new morning schedule looked like this:

8:00–8:30	Sort through in box, review and answer e-mail, write correspondence
8:30–9:00	Return phone calls
9:00–11:00	Work on priority project(s)
11:00–noon	Staff meeting

If you are constantly interrupted and cannot control your time this much, be sure to organize the time you can control. Work with your supervisor and coworkers to find ways to reduce interruptions. One proven method is to keep lists of issues you want to discuss with others, then meet with them at specific times once or twice a day for five minutes to answer questions and make new plans. These meetings are more productive and take less total time than interruptions that start with the question, "Have you got a minute?"

Getting organized is crucial to getting better control of your work activities. Once you have accomplished this, you can focus on completing your most important activities by prioritizing.

Prioritizing Your Tasks

On Friday afternoon or Monday morning, review your Master List and identify those tasks that must be completed in the coming work week. Designate these as "A" priorities and estimate the amount of time each one will take. Then schedule these tasks on those days of the week when time is available so that they will be accomplished by their deadlines.

Review your weekly tasks and deadlines with your supervisor to make sure there are no misunderstandings.

Designate tasks that must be completed within the next two to four weeks as "B" priorities and give them deadline dates. Designate all other tasks that are important enough to list but have no specific deadlines as "C" priorities.

You may find it helpful to keep your Master List on a word processor so you can group your tasks according to their priority and change your list each week as tasks are completed and priorities change.

Copy your appointments from your calendar to your daily to-do list. Using this combination of a prioritized Master List along with your calendar and a daily to-do list is helpful in two ways:

- You will not worry about forgetting important tasks and appointments, and you will have a plan to work on only the highest-value tasks during the week.

- You will be able to regain your focus quickly if you are interrupted by an unexpected task that takes an extended time to complete.

Having now gotten your work organized and tasks prioritized, there is one last key to managing your actions well—minimizing unproductive activities. Sometimes this can be the toughest challenge.

Take a Moment

Use the lines below to identify your A-, B-, and C-level tasks for the coming month.

A-Level Tasks:

____________ ____________ ____________

____________ ____________ ____________

B-Level Tasks:

____________ ____________ ____________

____________ ____________ ____________

C-Level Tasks:

____________ ____________ ____________

____________ ____________ ____________

Minimizing Unproductive Activities

Unproductive activities include some activities that we can control and many that we can't. Here are five steps to help reduce the amount of time we spend on each:

Unproductive activities include some activities that we can control and many that we can't.

- **Keep a time log for two weeks.**
  Keep track of how much time you spend in each of your major activities by quarter-hour increments. Your record doesn't have to be exact. Just stop every hour or two, think about what you've been doing, and write it down on your daily calendar.

  - **Example:** Correspondence ("C")—.25; Outbound Telephone Calls ("O T")—.25; Meetings ("M")—1.0.

  Be sure to log time spent in social conversations, looking for files, etc. These are activities you have some control over. Also, have codes for interruptions (keep track of who interrupts you most) and inbound phone calls. These are activities that are harder for you to control.

After two weeks, total up your time in each category and convert it to a percentage of your total time.

■ **Example:** C = 4.0 hours = 5%; O T = 3.0 hours = 4%; M = 10 hours = 13%.

Analyze how your time is being spent.

Analyze how your time is being spent. Look for the larger percentages and how much time you spend in meetings, conversations, and interruptions. These have the greatest potential for gaining more time for high-value activities. Show your supervisor a summary of your time usage and see if he or she can help reduce the number of meetings you must attend and the number of avoidable interruptions you have. Then plan tactful ways you can reduce your time in conversations with talkative coworkers.

Take a Moment

Keep a sample time log for the next full workday. Total up your percentages at the end of the day. Are you surprised by the results?

- **Negotiate priorities.**
  If you have multiple bosses with conflicting demands on your time, ask them to work out the priorities of your workload before giving you assignments.
- **Reduce phone time.**
  Work out an exchange with coworkers to cover your phone for specific blocks of time when you really need to concentrate without phone interruptions.
- **Manage deadlines.**
  When you get into a time crunch, change the deadlines you have personally set for yourself and negotiate new deadlines if they have been set by others.
- **Follow your plan.**
  Reduce your procrastination by following your plan and trying to beat budgeted times. Reward yourself when you do so in some nonfattening way.

One of the best ways of minimizing unproductive activities is delegating. Many times we spend time doing tasks that are important, but that could be done well enough by someone else.

Delegating Responsibilities

■ Taylor looked at the piles of work stacking up on her desk. She'd only been a supervisor for three months, and already she was falling behind. "I'll never get through all of this on my own," she moaned as she started to prioritize her unfinished tasks. "But whom can I get to help?"

Delegating is a powerful way to accomplish a number of important objectives because it:

- Gains more time for the supervisor.
- Focuses the supervisor on higher-value tasks.
- Helps motivate subordinates.
- Develops subordinates' capabilities.

However, delegating is hard for some supervisors. Here are several major reasons and some suggestions for overcoming each problem:

- **The supervisor prefers "doing" rather than "supervising."** This is common for new supervisors. If this is true of you, remember that *your* supervisor will evaluate your performance at least partially on how well you direct others. Start slowly by giving team members tasks you are certain they can accomplish. Assign more challenging tasks as they (and you) gain more confidence.

- **The supervisor believes he or she can do the tasks quicker or better than a subordinate.** This may be true. However, with proper training, your team members can learn the tasks well enough to complete them and, in time, may well do them quicker or better than you. Remember, part of your responsibility is to develop your people. Give them the opportunity to grow, the chance to do things their way (which may be different from yours), and the opportunity to learn from their mistakes.

Part of your responsibility is to develop your people.

◆ **The supervisor doesn't know how to delegate effectively.** Here are some tips that will make it easier:

Pick tasks to give each employee that fit her or his skills, personality type, and interests.

- Pick tasks to give each employee that fit her or his skills, personality type, and interests. For example, you might give scheduling to a detail-oriented person and give a team presentation to a forceful or more social person.
- Make sure employees know their tasks are important. Highlight how a task affects the department and the organization.
- Train employees using the following formula:
    1. **Tell them how it's done.** Find out what they already know then give them a logical explanation of how to accomplish the task well.
    2. **Show them how it's done.** Give a demonstration along with an explanation.
    3. **Let them do it while you watch.** Explain, encourage, and gently correct as they work.
- Follow up once or twice to give employees tips and positive reinforcement.

Take a Moment

Identify some tasks you can delegate and write them in the left-hand column below. In the right-hand column, list team members who you think could accomplish those tasks.

____________________	____________________
____________________	____________________
____________________	____________________

Delegation is one of the most powerful time-saving techniques you can use. It is also one of the best ways to reduce stress when your workload is high. Let's look at other ways you can reduce stress and improve the quality of your work life.

Managing Your Stress

Stress is normal, and even desirable up to a point. But when you feel tired, nervous, or overly distracted for more than a few days, you need to reduce your stress level. Fortunately, you can control your stress by developing a stress-management plan and making changes that will help you have a more balanced lifestyle.

You can begin to control your stress by recognizing the four basic levels of stress and how you react to each:

1. **Energized**—At this level, stress is positive and actually helps us to live a healthy, fulfilling life. For example, having new challenges, such as working toward a degree, getting a new job, or learning a different skill can be very positive. These cause us to use all of our abilities and to develop new ones. Here, stress generates a sense of adventure and optimism.

2. **Alarmed**—At this stage, stress can be an unexpected and unwelcome jolt or an accumulation of challenges that suddenly seems overwhelming. In either situation, our bodies respond as if threatened: blood pressure rises, adrenaline flows, and muscles tense for action. If it is a short-term jolt, these reactions help us prepare to deal with the situation. However, if it is an accumulation of continuing stressors, it can hurt our ability to function well in life and work.

3. **Resistant**—This is a continuation of the alarmed stage of stress beyond several days. During this stage, a person may begin to deny that he or she is having stress problems, try to close out negative feelings, or narrow the scope of his or her activities. All of this is an attempt to handle problems that cannot be quickly or easily solved.

4. **Exhausted**—If the situation continues and the body stays in a constant state of alarm beyond several weeks, a person may experience an increasing number of symptoms, such as:
   - Poor sleep habits
   - Lower productivity
   - Unusual behavior
   - Depression and anxiety
   - Hypertension and irritability
   - Illness

Recognizing that we are beyond a healthy level of stress is critical to correcting the situation. At this point, we can develop a plan to regain balance and reduce stress.

Creating a Plan to Reduce Stress

Follow these two steps to successfully reduce stress in your life:

Step 1: Identify the High Stressors in Your Life

Sometimes, if you are experiencing Stage 3 or Stage 4 stress, you may not recognize exactly what is bothering you. Consider the following four areas of life that psychologists say are the main causes of continuing stress. Then write down the specific issues in each area that bother you most:

- Lack of time

  ____

  ____

  ____

- Upsetting relationships

  ____

  ____

  ____

- Lack of direction

  ____

  ____

  ____

◆ Trying to be perfect

____

____

____

Next write as many specifics as you can for the four most common stress areas on the job:

◆ Workload (too much or too little)

____

____

____

◆ Compensation

____

____

____

◆ Conflict with the boss or coworkers

____

____

____

◆ Unchallenging work

____

____

____

Now put a check mark by the stress areas that are the most bothersome for you. With this as a basis, you can now plan actions to reduce your stress.

Step 2: Develop a Plan for Addressing the Stressors You Have Identified

Some things can't be resolved quickly, but you can begin to take small steps toward positive changes. Just having a plan will give you a greater feeling of control, and that will help reduce your stress.

Just having a plan will give you a greater feeling of control, and that will help reduce your stress.

As you develop your plan, keep in mind that there are three possible responses to any stressor:

- **Change the stressor.**
  If you have some level of control over your stressful circumstances, develop a plan to reduce or eliminate the problems, as in the following examples:

  - Bill was the manager of a college bookstore. He hated placing orders for a particular professor because the professor was always intimidating and unpleasant to work with. When Bill considered the situation, he decided he could change it in one of two ways: He could try to stop interacting with the professor by asking another employee to take his orders, refusing to return his calls, or changing jobs, or he could learn to communicate more assertively and train the professor to treat him differently. He decided on the latter option and began to stand up for himself more assertively when dealing with the professor.

  - Salvatore felt trapped in his job. The position provided no challenge for him and didn't pay very well, and he saw no way to advance. After some thinking, he developed a plan for how he could acquire the training needed to qualify for higher-level jobs.

  The key to changing a stressful situation is to focus on one or two goals, then develop a realistic plan to achieve them. Involve others, such as your supervisor, human resources professionals, friends, or counselors who can give you good advice. Your plan and their support will make a big difference in reducing your stress.

Sometimes you have no control over the stressors affecting you. In this situation, you still have control over one critical element—how you react. You can learn how to change your reaction to be more positive and less stressful.

- **Change your response to the stressor.**
  This is primarily a mental challenge that will require you to change how you think about the stressor. Psychologists know that emotions are mainly generated by thoughts. They also know most people can control their thoughts far more than they know. Start by examining your internal *self-talk* when you are feeling very stressed. What are you thinking about when you feel that way?

In our self-talk, we judge our circumstances and the behavior of other people as well as ourselves. When that judgment is negative, we often use the word "should." For example, if someone speaks harshly to you, you might think, "She shouldn't talk to me that way," or "What I should have said to him was . . . ." Many times, changing key words in your internal dialogue can help lessen your negative feelings about situations. In the previous example, you could change the word "should" to "could." Then you could say to yourself, "She could be much more positive in talking to me." This does not eliminate the problem, but it makes it feel less serious and less personal.

In our self-talk, we judge our circumstances and the behavior of other people as well as ourselves.

Another way of mentally changing your reaction to a stressful situation or another person's negative comments is to ask yoursef questions, such as, "What can I learn about dealing with this person in the future from this conversation?" or "What is causing her to act this way?" This puts us into a more objective frame of mind. Being more objective reduces emotion and helps us to feel more in control.

Negative emotions are the result of negative thoughts. Identifying your own negative thoughts and then substituting more positive or productive thoughts can help tremendously in reducing stress. Talking things through with a friend can help you identify your negative thoughts. However, someone who is in the third or fourth stage of stress may need the help of a professional counselor.

Negative emotions are the result of negative thoughts.

In addition to our mental response, we can change our physical response to help reduce the negative effects of stress.

◆ **Counteract the effects of the stressor.**
There are many ways to offset the negative effects of stress. Here are a few suggestions:

- **Exercise.** Ask your doctor for advice about how to exercise appropriately for your age and current physical condition. Even light exercise can help tremendously. Go slowly and schedule short exercise periods to begin with. Your doctor might also be able to prescribe medication and changes in your diet that will help lessen your stress symptoms.

- **Take short breaks.** Every hour or so, walk around; breathe deeply several times; and massage your jaw, neck, and shoulders to reduce tension. Learn relaxation techniques and use them regularly while you are working.

Learn relaxation techniques and use them regularly while you are working.

- **Take up a hobby.** Either find a new one or go back to an old one. The idea is to do something that you truly enjoy that distracts you from life and work challenges. The distraction helps reduce your focus on negative things and brings more balance to your perspective.

- **Find things to laugh at.** One of the casualties of stress can be your sense of humor. Make a point of looking for humor—in newspaper cartoons, books, movies, and television. Laughing has great power to reduce stress both physically and mentally.

- **Read and listen to motivational messages in books and audiotapes.** These can give you positive messages to substitute for the negative messages you are receiving from yourself and others. In a way, they help reprogram your thinking.

There are many other ways to counteract the negative effects of stress. The key is to look for them, consult with others, and develop a plan. Once you have a plan, implement it as soon as possible. Delay will only allow the problems to continue and make them seem increasingly harder to deal with.

Chapter Summary

An important part of your new role as supervisor is learning to manage your time and your stress. Three key techniques that will help you manage your time are organizing your work, prioritizing your tasks, and minimizing unproductive activities.

Another technique that will help you manage your time and reduce your stress is to delegate some of your responsibilities to others. Delegating will help you gain more time and allow you to focus on higher-value tasks. It will also help motivate your employees and develop their capabilities.

You may find that your new responsibilities bring increasing levels of stress. We can identify four progressive levels of stress: energized, alarmed, resistant, and exhausted.

To reduce your stress, you need to identify the high stressors in your life and then develop a plan for addressing them. You can deal with any stressor by changing it, changing your response to it, or counteracting its negative effects.

Self-Check: Chapter 8 Review

Answers to the following questions appear on page 124.

1. What are the three keys to managing your time?

   a. ______________________________

   b. ______________________________

   c. ______________________________

2. Two key ways to get organized are getting rid of

   ____________ and ______________ your tasks.

3. When prioritizing, how would you define the following levels of tasks?

   A-level task: ______________________________

   B-level task: ______________________________

   C-level task: ______________________________

4. When delegating tasks, you should assign tasks that fit each

   employee's _______________, _______________

   _______________, and _______________.

5. Match each of the stages of stress listed below with its description.

_____ Energized
_____ Alarmed
_____ Resistant
_____ Exhausted

a. Stress lasts for several days. A person may begin to deny he orshe is having stress problems, try to close out negative feelings, or narrow the scope of his or her activities.

b. Stress appears as an unexpected jolt or the accumulation of challenges that suddenly seem overwhelming. The body responds as if threatened.

c. The body stays in a constant state of alarm beyond several weeks, leading to a variety of symptoms, such as poor sleep habits and depression.

d. At this level, stress is positive and actually helps people to live healthy, fulfilling lives.

6. What are two important steps you can take to reduce stress?

a. ____

b. ____

Chapter *Nine*

Growing into Management

Chapter Objectives

- ▶ Understand what managers do.
- ▶ Know what skills to develop in order to qualify for greater responsibility.

In Chapter 1, we considered a diagram of the career steps leading from nonsupervisory positions to supervision to management. The diagram showed that the further up in the organization you go, the greater the scope and depth of your duties. Let's look more specifically at the key responsibilities of managers:

- Managers are often responsible for one or more organizational units that have significant impact on the operation or the financial well-being of the organization. If they do their job well, there is a noticeable positive effect. But the opposite is also true. If they don't perform well, there is a noticeable negative effect. This shows in reduced revenue or profit, increases in customer or employee complaints, or delays in delivery of products or services.

A manager's role is often that of advisor who helps supervisors work more effectively with their subordinates.

- Managers often supervise people who supervise others. Their role many times is that of advisor who helps supervisors work more effectively with their subordinates. This can mean acting as a coach to the supervisor and sometimes being a mediator between the supervisor and his or her employee. This also means that managers need to have a good understanding of employment laws and potential liabilities to the organization.

- Managers develop the plans and budgets for their areas of responsibility and do all that is possible to meet or exceed their objectives. This often calls for innovative solutions to unforeseen problems. Managers are expected to handle the unexpected and still deliver results.

- Managers are responsible for communicating the mission and the culture of the organization to everyone in their areas of responsibility. They are the main link between the organization's strategic planners and its deliverers of products and services.

Understanding these key responsibilities will help you know what you must learn to advance into management. But there are also important skill areas that you will need to develop in order to become a successful manager.

Developing Skills to Become a Manager

One of the best ways to qualify for greater responsibility is to solve problems effectively. This means recognizing problems when and even before they occur, then developing ways to correct or overcome them. To the extent that you can develop solutions before your manager asks you to, you are demonstrating an important managerial skill.

One of the best ways to qualify for greater responsibility is to solve problems effectively.

There are other skills that you need to develop to advance in the organization. Here are five key abilities you need to develop to become a successful manager:

- **Communication**
  This topic was discussed in Chapter 3; however, its importance cannot be overemphasized. The higher up you go in management, the more time you spend communicating with others on the phone, face-to-face, and in meetings. Studies have shown that the percentage of time spent communicating increases to almost 80 percent in senior management positions. It is important to understand that people are often initially promoted to supervision because of their technical capabilities. However, supervisors who keep advancing not only keep their technical skills sharp but also develop their abilities to listen for complete understanding; involve others in the decision-making process; and speak clearly, tactfully, and persuasively.

Being able to speak well does not necessarily give someone the ability to write well.

- **Writing**
This is another form of communication; however, it calls for a different set of skills. Being able to speak well does not necessarily give someone the ability to write well. In writing, as in speaking, one needs to be clear, positive, and tactful. One must also be concise, use good grammar, and display a good vocabulary. This is critical to a writer because communication written on paper or stored in a computer can survive for an indefinite period. Also, writing is a primary way of persuading others to accept your ideas or buy your products and services. Those who develop their writing skills tend to excel beyond those who don't.

- **Financial understanding**
Every business has particular financial measures that are key indicators of the well-being of the organization. These might include sales conversion percentages, number of units shipped per week, total volume of back orders, and others. Those who understand which financial measures are the most critical to their organization and how these measures can be positively affected are in an excellent position to help the organization when opportunities arise. This, in turn, helps those individuals' advancement potential.

- **Ability to manage change**
Change occurs at an ever-increasing rate. The ability to adapt at an individual level and to help others learn to change is becoming more important each year. Some of this ability is based in personality style and attitude, but it is definitely something that can be developed by learning how to analyze changes objectively and how to be more patient and positive with yourself and others.

Those who keep advancing are open to new ideas, willing to admit mistakes, and actively searching for new information.

- **Willingness to learn**
Too many supervisors and managers seem to reach a level where they seem unwilling to grow. They act as if they already know it all or as if they are afraid of admitting there are things they don't know. Continuing to learn is a skill that can be developed. Those who keep advancing are open to new ideas, willing to admit mistakes, and actively searching for new information. They are more valuable to the organization because they help keep it competitive and help it find more opportunities.

This is not a complete list; however, it gives you a good basis for assessing where you need to focus your self-development efforts. Your advancement is your responsibility. The more preparation you have, the more likely you will be able to take advantage of opportunities when they arise. The fact that you have read this book is a good indicator that you are the kind of person who takes responsibility for your own success. With that trait and your continued self-development efforts, your success is assured.

Congratulations and good luck.

Chapter Summary

The further up the organization you advance, the greater the scope and depth of your duties. Managers are often responsible for one or more organizational units that have significant impact on the operation or financial well-being of the organization. Managers often supervise people who supervise others, develop the plans and budgets for their areas of responsibility, and do all that is possible to meet or exceed their objectives.

The ability to solve problems effectively is a key skill for becoming a manager. Other important skills managers need to develop include:

1. Communication
2. Writing
3. Financial understanding
4. Ability to manage change
5. Willingness to learn

Posttest

So now how do you feel about being a supervisor? Have you identified your areas of strength and skills you need to develop? Let's take a moment and see how well you have done.

This survey is similar to the self-assessment you completed at the beginning of the book, only with different questions. Read each statement and then circle the number that most closely describes your current skill level according the following scale: 1 = Strongly disagree, 2 = Disagree, 3 = Not sure, 4 = Agree, 5 = Strongly agree.

1. I understand how my new duties as a supervisor differ from my prior jobs and know what I need to do.	1	2	3	4	5
2. I understand the biggest frustrations of my job and have a good idea of how to handle them.	1	2	3	4	5
3. I know the key elements of being a good coach and team leader.	1	2	3	4	5
4. I know from my employees' point of view what is important to them in their work.	1	2	3	4	5
5. I know the listening skills that I need to work on to fully understand the other person's view.	1	2	3	4	5
6. I avoid giving mixed signals with my words, voice tone, and body language when I talk with others.	1	2	3	4	5

7. I plan how I approach people based on their personality style and other information I know about them.	1	2	3	4	5
8. I know how to conduct effective meetings.	1	2	3	4	5
9. I know the best sources to use in gathering information before making a decision.	1	2	3	4	5
10. I understand how to avoid focusing too quickly on one "obvious" solution to a problem.	1	2	3	4	5
11. I know what to do when I come into conflict with peers and former peers who now work for me.	1	2	3	4	5
12. I understand my role in discipline and what responsibility employees have in the process.	1	2	3	4	5
13. I understand how to make progressive discipline a more positive process.	1	2	3	4	5
14. I know how to conduct a termination meeting in a way that minimizes stress and potential problems.	1	2	3	4	5
15. I have a clear understanding of what sexual harassment is and how to avoid it.	1	2	3	4	5

16. I understand my responsibilities and employees' rights under OSHA.	1	2	3	4	5
17. I understand how to organize my work and prioritize my tasks.	1	2	3	4	5
18. I know how to minimize my unproductive activities.	1	2	3	4	5
19. I know the benefits and action steps of delegating.	1	2	3	4	5
20. I understand clearly what managers do and the areas I need to develop in order to advance.	1	2	3	4	5

Now, add up the numbers you circled and compare your total to the table below:

60 or less—You're still unclear about your new job as a supervisor. Focus on your five lowest-rated statements and look again at the chapters they refer to.

61 to 80—You have a good understanding about your job as a supervisor. Look at your lowest-rated statements and review the chapters they refer to so you can develop even greater confidence.

81 to 100—You are very confident in your understanding of your job as supervisor. Focus on the areas you need to keep developing so you can be well prepared to meet your supervisory challenges and seize new opportunities when they arise.

How did you do compared to the self-assessment you completed at the beginning of the book? Chances are good that your total ratings were much improved. Continue referring to this book and take advantage of as many other supervisory and management development resources as you can. The more knowledge you gain in these areas, the more you help yourself achieve both your career and life goals.

Answers to Chapter Reviews

Chapter 1 (pages 18 and 19)

1. The higher in the organization you go, the greater the scope and depth of your duties.

2. c. Nonsupervisor
   a. Supervisor
   b. Manager

3. Choose from:
   - Coaching and motivating employees
   - Getting employees to work together as a team
   - Solving problems with others
   - Managing conflicts between others
   - Counseling and disciplining
   - Managing your time as well as that of others
   - Conducting meetings
   - Dealing with your stress and the stress of others

4. a. Feeling overwhelmed
   b. Jealousy from former coworkers
   c. Lack of respect
   d. Frustration with bureaucracy

Chapter 2 (pages 29 and 30)

1. Both are short-term motivators. Money incentives are effective only for the time they are given; fear is effective only as long as the supervisor is immediately present.

2. Choose from:
   - Give employees sincere compliments on their work.
   - Ask employees for their opinions on business issues.
   - Give employees special projects.
   - Communicate about what's going on.
   - Cross-train employees in other jobs.
   - Set goals with individuals about their performance and their development.

3. c. Forceful
   d. Social
   a. Steady
   b. Detailed

4. Choose from:
   - Certificates
   - Inexpensive plaques or trophies
   - Coffee cups
   - Lunches
   - A small amount of paid time off
   - Drawings for prizes

5. Choose from:
   - Fairness
   - Calmness
   - A positive attitude
   - Willingness to listen
   - Patience
   - Knowledge

6. a. Set teamwork goals together.
   b. Hold regular meetings with the team.
   c. Develop a team identity.

Chapter 3 (pages 45 and 46)

1. b. Hearing
   a. Listening

2. b. Could or would

3. Communicating effectively means using your tone of voice to <u>support</u> your verbal message.

4. You are interested in what the other person has to say.

5. You are open to the other person.

6. c. Forceful
   a. Social
   b. Steady
   d. Detailed

7. a. Hold only those meetings that are necessary to communicate to all parties involved.
   b. Always have an agenda.
   c. Lead assertively.
   d. Send meeting minutes out within 24 hours.

Chapter 4 (page 57)

1. When gathering information about a problem, ask questions that begin with who, what, when, where, why, and how.

2. a. People closest to the problem
   b. Experts
   c. Personal research

3. a. List all the reasons against a solution.
   b. Brainstorm other options.
   c. Ask Why? at least five times for each possible cause of the problem.

4. a. Organizational culture
   b. Politics
   c. Economic climate

5. Follow up

Chapter 5 (page 69)

1. Because of their need for control and directness, Forceful people sometimes interrupt others, hurry conversations, give orders without explanation, and are overly blunt. Social people like to talk and have positive interaction. They can become frustrated when they aren't allowed to express themselves and may feel that the Forceful person is being insensitive and rude.

2. a. Physical factors
   b. Mental factors

3. Conflicting goals and competition

4. a. How does that person threaten me or my goals?
   b. How do I threaten that person?

5. a. The conflict could hurt the productivity and morale of your department.
   b. Your credibility with your other employees could be hurt.

Chapter 6 (page 81)

1. The purpose of discipline is to <u>change behavior</u>, not to <u>punish</u>.

2. a. Be consistent and fair.
   b. Don't wait to see if things improve.
   c. Document specific problem behavior.

3. a. Who did it?
   b. What did he or she do or say?
   c. When did he or she do or say it?
   d. Where did the incident occur?

4. a. Examine your own attitude.
   b. Use a checklist to prepare for your meeting.
   c. Use positive language.

5. F = Facts
   O = Objectives
   S = Solutions
   A = Actions
   \+ = Extra efforts

Chapter 7 (pages 92 and 93)

1. The Civil Rights Act of 1964, Title VII prohibits discrimination on the basis of race, sex, or religion. It resulted in the creation of the Equal Employment Opportunity Commission (EEOC).

2. a. Quid pro quo sexual harassment
   b. Hostile environment sexual harassment

3. b. Explanation: Ignoring harassment is not an effective way to deal with it. Speak up assertively when someone else's behavior makes you uncomfortable.

4. c. Explanation: OSHA and state safety inspectors have the right to inspect workplaces without notice periodically and to talk with employees without a supervisor being present.

5. To avoid discriminating against job applicants, job application and interview questions should focus on the applicant's experience and ability to do the job.

6. The employee could have grounds for a wrongful discharge suit. The employee could also file a discrimination suit if he or she is a member of a protected group.

Chapter 8 (pages 110 and 111)

1. a. Organize your work.
   b. Prioritize your tasks.
   c. Minimize unproductive activities.

2. Two key ways to get organized are getting rid of clutter and scheduling your tasks.

3. A-level task: Must be completed in the coming week
   B-level task: Must be completed in two to four weeks
   C-level task: No specific deadline

4. When delegating tasks, you should assign tasks that fit each employee's skills, personality type, and interests.

5. d. Energized
   b. Alarmed
   a. Resistant
   c. Exhausted

6. a. Identify the high stressors in your life.
   b. Develop a plan for addressing the stressors you have identified.